UR-INE TROUBLE

Kent Holtorf, M.D.

Editor
Stephanie Cartozian

Vandalay Press
Scottsdale, Arizona

Printed in the United States of America

Publisher's Cataloging-in-Publication

Holtorf, Kent
     Ur-ine trouble : the truth about drug tests : why drug users are passing and non-users are failing / Kent Holtorf ; editor Stephanie Cartozian. -- 1st ed.
     p. cm
     Includes bibliographical references and index.
     ISBN: 0-9657467-4-7

     1. Drug testing. I. Title. II. Title: You're in trouble III. Title: Urine trouble

RM301.63.H65 1998   658.3822
                                       QBI97-41624

Acknowledgments

I would like to thank Angelen VanDaele and Tom Arthur for their heroic generosity and patience, and Dr. Steve Haase for his support and direction.

I would also like to thank my family: Mom, Dad, Don Jr., Kurt, Andrea, Donnie, and Coleen.

I would like to especially thank Stephanie Cartozian. I am deeply indebted to Stephanie. This book could not have been written without her inspiration, encouragement, and assistance. Her guidance and profound wisdom have made an enormous impact on my life.

About the Author

Kent Holtorf, M.D. received a B.S. in kinesiology at The University of California at Los Angeles. He then completed his doctoral training at St. Louis University School of Medicine. He trained in general medicine and anesthesiology at Harbor County Medical Center and at U.C.L.A. Center for Health Sciences.

For years, he has presented scientific facts and data that has forced drug testing experts to reexamine their testing practices and techniques and to privately concede to the inadequacies of drug testing. Since completing his research, Dr. Holtorf has spoken with hundreds of people whose lives have been devastated by the inaccuracies of drug testing. He has also served as a Drug Testing Expert in high profile court cases.

Dr. Holtorf has discussed drug testing on numerous nationally syndicated radio and television talk shows and has been a featured guest on the *Dr. Dean Edell Show*, the *ABC News Health Report,* and the *Howard Stern Show.* He is an internationally recognized drug testing expert, being quoted in newspapers nationwide and abroad.

Contents

Warning-Disclaimer

The Drug Testing Fallacy

The general public has been led to believe that mass drug testing is an effective means by which to deter and treat illicit drug use and has rallied behind employment drug testing as a fundamental part of the "War on Drugs". But no well done study has shown that preemployment drug testing decreases drug use, provides a safer workplace, or is financially beneficial to the employer. Ironically, drug testing violates the rights of the members in the society of which it is designed to protect; it diverts energy and resources from legitimate, productive programs that can actually help to decrease drug use; and its punitive nature deters people from seeking the assistance they need. The United States is spending over 1.2 billion dollars per year (not including money spent on time lost from work attributable to the testing process or the cost for recruitment of replacement workers) without any or negligible benefit other than a symbolic one (178). Objective biomedical science tells us that drug testing is of no established value in coping with illicit drug use. It has been called a form of chemical McCarthyism (16) that makes us a nation of suspects. Urine screening is a probe to identify deviance, not dysfunction; a technique to investigate humans, not performance (17). Indiscriminate and mass screening does a disservice to the community and to the society that it is designed to help, but the societal need to fight the "War on Drugs" in any manner possible has served as justification for all the far reaching negative consequences of drug testing. People should understand what price is being asked for the perception that something is being done and be quick to say they will not pay it (4).

The implementation of drug testing is proving to be ineffective at deterring drug use and is not providing any cost benefits for employers. After an exhaustive review of the scientific literature in 1995, the National Academy of Sciences found "there is as yet no conclusive scientific evidence from properly controlled studies that employment drug-testing programs widely discourage

drug use or encourage rehabilitation. (178)."
Subcommittees of the National Research Council and the
Institute of Medicine involved in the research state that
much of the data used to justify drug testing is flawed, or
at least of dubious statistical power, and they conclude
that "despite beliefs to the contrary, the preventative
effects of drug-testing programs have never been
adequately demonstrated." Drug testing proponents often
refer to a few poorly designed studies that show
employment drug testing offers some economic benefit to
employers. But every study that is used to justify claims
of economic benefit has not been accepted for publication
in a reputable peer reviewed journal. They have serious
flaws in their study designs with erroneous results
distorted by faulty assumptions, subtle biases, flawed
calculations, and confounding variables. Conclusions
based on these poorly done studies are clearly invalid
(178).

From information provided by the California Drug Abuse
Information and Monitoring Project, officers of a
governmental appointed task force set up to evaluate drug
testing doubted that the high costs of drug testing would
justify its marginal theoretical benefits (14). A
congressional survey of drug testing revealed that it cost
$11.7 million to test 28,772 federal employees between

1989-1990, which resulted in 153 positive tests (15). Thus, it cost $76,000 to find each positive testing urine, of which the majority were allegedly false positive specimens (a urine that tests positive due to something other than illicit drugs). An electronic manufacturer arrived at a similarly exorbitant cost of $20,000 per positive test (205). Furthermore, if a company actually wanted to try and rid their company of "hard" drug users, it would, based on the pharmacokinetics of the "hard" drugs, have to test employees at least 2 to 3 times per week. This would cost several hundred times more than the standard rate of 1 to 2 random tests per year and would most likely be deemed unaffordable by even the largest of corporations.

The International Labor Organization (ILO) stated in 1993 that "there might appear to be several reasons or objectives for employers to establish testing programs, but empirical evidence from scientific studies is largely inconclusive as to whether those objectives are likely to be achieved (205)...Unfortunately, much of the evaluation that has been completed on workplace testing has been anecdotal and non-experimental, allowing for little confidence in the results. Thus, the present state appears to be that valid scientific documentation of the beneficial effects of any testing program with regard to the goals for such programs is generally lacking (206)."

Research also shows that drug testing does not result in decreased absenteeism, workplace accidents, or disability claims. A recent survey in 1996 among 961 companies that tested more than 500,000 applicants and 196,000 workers conducted by a leading management group showed that drug testing was ineffective at deterring drug use or at decreasing absenteeism, illness, or disability claims. "Costs have increased tenfold since 1990 with very little statistical evidence of results," said Eric Greenberg, who conducted the survey for the American Management Association. Increasing numbers of companies are terminating their drug testing programs because of its failure to provide cost saving benefits (179). Similarly, the Business Department at the University of Wisconsin examined 4 years of employee accident and illness records at 48 firms and compared the companies that had drug testing programs to those who did not. They found no difference in accidents or illness rates.

Arthur J. McBay Ph.D., Chief Toxicologist and Professor of Pathology and Pharmacy at the University of North Carolina and Chief Medical Examiner for the State of North Carolina, also agrees and states, "Industries that use testing programs and the advocates who sell such programs are quoted in the media to the effect that significant improvements in the drug problem have followed the introduction of these programs. However, no data or documentation is offered describing the extent of the problem before and after drug testing (10)." In addition, "I have seen no evidence that any of the urine testing programs have had a beneficial effect on the health, safety, or productivity of the Armed Services or any other group tested (208)."

Diana Walsh from the Harvard School of Public Health writes, "Drug testing in the workplace presents a striking case of a policy instrument that has penetrated fast and far, accompanied by almost no credible scientific warrant of effectiveness (9)." The American Medical Association recognizes this fact and does not recommend the widespread use of drug testing or the testing of doctors (11). The American Academy of Pediatrics also "strenuously opposes" the drug testing of children, adolescents, and teens. The American Academy of Pediatrics Committee on Substance Abuse states in the August 1996 edition of the medical journal *Pediatrics* that drug abuse among children, adolescents, and adults is an issue of national importance, but the solution to the drug problem is not drug testing. They concluded that involuntary testing is not appropriate (even with parental consent), and "students and student athletes should not be singled out for involuntary screening for drugs of abuse. Such testing should not be a condition for participation in sports or any school functions...(180)"

Drug testing also unfairly targets the least dangerous of recreationally used drugs, marijuana. Many who use marijuana on a periodic basis are switching to "harder" drugs that don't last in the system as long. For instance, after the Navy implemented drug testing, there was a "notable shift to increased alcohol use" (173), which correlates with increased workplace accidents and decreased productivity, and LSD is said to have become the illicit drug of choice in the military due to its relative undetectability (221). It was shown that when England and Wales implemented the drug testing of prisoners, use of marijuana decreased but the use of harder drugs such as heroin almost doubled (208).

Companies that perform random drug testing are finding they often lose their best and most valued employees to positive tests due to common foods, over-the-counter preparations and prescription medications or due to occasional marijuana use during non-working hours. This is especially true of those companies whose policy it is to test employees receiving promotions. In addition, with the unemployment rate being at an all time low, employers now have fewer numbers of applicants to choose from, making it difficult and expensive to find a replacement. The time and money it takes to find a suitable replacement can be substantial. Charles Carroll, CEO of ASSET, which contracts with companies to infiltrate the workplace in search of employee drug abuse, states that there has been a dramatic change by companies in the way they are dealing with those who test positive to avoid losing some of their most valuable and productive employees. He says even Fortune 500 companies are becoming "softer" with their policies. For example, workers are being suspended and quickly brought back after second and third drug offenses rather than being fired. This does not mean that they are going to expensive and time consuming rehabilitation programs. Companies are being warned that they can't reverse their drug testing policies overnight without risking discrimination lawsuits (192). Also, when considering the implementation of a drug testing program, employers must also consider its affects on employee moral. For example, Tom Peters of *Bay Area Business* magazine states, if "future competitiveness depends upon treating people as an important part of the institution, the least respectful thing I can imagine doing to a human being is telling him to piss in a bottle once a month (174)."

Louis Maltby, Vice President of Drexelbrooks Engineering, decided not to do any drug testing. He argued, "We just don't think you need to test to keep the workplace drug-free. After all, drugs are just a symptom of something else. What you really want is a committed, dedicated workforce, people who like their jobs and care enough not to come to work stoned. What we do is select and nurture employees who are going to do a good job. We think if we do that, the drug problem takes care of itself. We're incredibly careful about the people we hire. You're saying you can have a drug testing program and have the kind of relations I'm talking about. I say you can't. The two are inimical. Ours is based on a relationship that doesn't come from a paycheck. When you say to an employee, ' You're doing a great job, but just the same I want you to pee in this jar and I'm sending someone to watch you,' you're undermining that trust (175)."

Published in the *Journal of General Internal Medicine* is a study by David C. Parish, M.D. from the Department of Internal Medicine at Mercy University School of Medicine, which evaluated workplace impairment due to drug use. He screened new hospital employees for drugs but kept the results confidential. Twelve percent of new employees tested positive for drug use. At the end of the year, there were "no differences in job performance between drug positive and drug negative employees." In fact, eleven drug negative employees were fired and no drug positive employees were fired (23).

In a study done by the National Institute on Drug Abuse at two utility companies, the Utah Power and Light Company ant the Georgia Power Company, Utah Power and Light "spent $215 per employee per year less on drug abusers in health insurance benefits than on the control group." Employees who tested positive at Georgia Power had a higher promotion rate than the company average, and workers that tested positive only for marijuana were absent 30% less often than average (194). In a similar study, Southern Electric International compared the rate of promotion, demotion, absenteeism, and sick leave between employees who tested positive and negative, and there was no significant difference (215). A 1988 Department of Transportation study found "No statistical conclusion regarding the relationship between drug use and...accidents were possible (219)."

Also, conflicting with the general public's assumption that marijuana negatively affects workers' performance are the findings of a study by N. Mello Ph.D. and J. Mendelson, Ph.D. This study allowed workers a choice of buying marijuana or tobacco cigarettes. Those who bought marijuana cigarettes, with some smoking up to 20 per day, either showed no change in productivity or an increase in work output with periods of maximal work coinciding with periods of maximal marijuana smoking (22). Other studies show similar results: Carlin and Trupin found daily marijuana smokers performed significantly faster than nonsmokers on tests of rapid visuomotor, scanning, tracking, and set-shifting, and Grant found that better performance on a variety of tasks actually correlated with heavy marijuana use (176). The National Research Council and the Institute of Medicine stated in 1995 that "it has not been demonstrated with any certainty that, in commonly used doses, any of the widely abused drugs significantly impact job performance (178)." Likewise, a 1990 study by the U.S. Department of Labor was unable to determine conclusively that workplace drug abuse is having a detrimental impact on employers (215).

Americans must realize that employment drug testing is being sold to them. The multibillion dollar drug testing industry aggressively peddles its wares and vigorously defends its lucrative industry. The overwhelming majority of drug testing experts and researchers are employed by the drug testing industry and have vested interests in promoting drug testing. This self promotion assures their livelihood but makes them incapable of objectively assessing the effects of drug testing. They have become paid lobbyists for the drug testing industry. Craig Zwerling, M.D. notes in the *Journal of the American Medical Association* that "a large industry of drug testers has arisen with a financial stake in expanding the market for workplace drug tests. The industry includes the companies that manufacture the equipment and chemicals used in drug testing, the laboratories that carry out the tests, the companies that collect the urine specimens, the medical review officers (MRO's) who review the test results, and the consultants who advise companies on drug testing. All these groups have worked together with the federal government to promote workplace drug testing (193)."

Even though drug testing does not result in a safer workplace with a decreased number of accidents or workers' compensation claims, insurance companies continue to promote post-accident drug testing. So if an employee loses an arm in an industrial accident or an employee injures her back on the job, he or she is immediately drug tested. Those individuals whose tests turn up positive are subsequently denied all health benefits. It doesn't matter if they tested positive from an illicit drug taken weeks earlier, or from the various foods, over-the-counter preparations or prescription medications that can cause a false positive test. They will immediately lose their job and their health benefits, and subsequently, the government will also deny them all unemployment benefits. Insurance companies are saving millions of dollars at the expense of innocent people. There is little risk of legal repercussions from employees who have been unjustly denied benefits because courts have ruled that drug tests need not be 100% accurate, but merely have a general scientific basis. Thus, in order to win punitive damages, one must prove that the insurance company intentionally engendered a false positive result to deny a non-drug user benefits. Without the possibility punitive damage awards, attorneys are unwilling to take these cases. Thus, there is little recourse for the person who has been unjustly labeled a drug user with subsequent loss of employment and all medical and unemployment benefits for his or her family. In fact, it often takes a court order to obtain documentation of the testing procedures and methods used on the sample, making it almost impossible for the average worker to challenge a positive result.

Politicians promote widespread drug testing not only to appear "hard" on drugs, but also to serve their major political backers. The drug testing industry contributes huge sums of money to the campaigns of the politicians who successfully promote their products. The powerful American Drug Use Testing Association aggressively lobbies at the state and local levels for legislation that will expand its markets. The politicians often knowingly regurgitate false and misleading information from the drug testing corporations' sales brochures to the American people as if it were fact. Eric D. Wish, M.D., Director of the Center for Substance Abuse Research at the University of Maryland, is highly critical of the way the government and the drug testing industry have falsified statistics to promote a sense of urgency to justify their political agendas. He states, "What is not so obvious is that the federal agencies that produce these statistics are also agents of the administration in power, and are not immune from pressures to interpret national drug statistics consistent with the ruling administration's view (187)." The Nevada Senate has helped increase the revenue of their major financial backers with the passing of the Nevada Senate Bill 371(Section 26.2), which mandates that insurance companies give employers who perform drug testing a 5% discount on health insurance premiums. This is designed to help the drug testing industry sell itself to the business community.

The government was not a major driving force behind private-sector employment drug testing until 1988. While the military had done some limited drug testing in the 1970's, and President Ronald Reagan set the stage for the drug testing of federal employees when he signed the "Drug-Free Workplace Order" in 1986, mandated private sector testing wasn't launched until the "Drug-Free workplace Act" was signed in 1988. This required that any business or institution receiving $25,000 or more per year in federal funds-directly or indirectly-have in place a drug testing program (197).

To justify the mandating of private sector testing, President George Bush declared in 1989 that "drug abuse among American workers costs businesses anywhere from $60 billion to $100 billion a year in lost productivity, absenteeism, drug-related accidents, medical claims, and theft." This number has been promulgated and arbitrarily increased as time goes on by drug testing proponents and has served as the basis for the justification for employment drug testing (194).

The numbers grew out of a survey of 3,700 households by the research Triangle Institute (RTI) in 1982 that found that the average income of households with at least one person who admitted having ever used marijuana daily (20 days or more in a 30-day period) was 28 percent lower than the average reported income of otherwise similar households. The RTI researchers defined that difference in income as "loss due to marijuana use"; the total loss, when extrapolated to the general population, came to $26 billion. The researchers then added on the estimated costs of drug-related crime, health problems and accidents to arrive at a grand total of $47 billion for "costs to society from drug abuse." This figure, "adjusted" to account for inflation and population increase, represents the basis of the president's statement, according to Henrick J. Harwood, who headed the RTI study and then went to work for the White House's Drug-Policy Office (194).

The RTI survey included questions on current drug use (at least once within the past month). but according to Harwood there was no significant difference between the income of households with current users of illegal drugs and the income of otherwise similar households. Thus, if the government's conclusions about the "costs to society from drug abuse" are to be believed, then one must also conclude that it would be beneficial for individuals who had used marijuana in the past, but do not currently use drugs, to start using "hard" drugs. This should, based on the government's interpretation of the study, lead to greater earnings. When asked if that meant that current use of even hard drugs, as opposed to a single marijuana binge in the distant past, does not lead to any economic loss? Harwood replied, "You would be on safe ground saying that." Obviously, this flawed study did not demonstrate "costs to society from drug abuse" at all. It was merely the Bush administration misrepresenting the study findings to justify the escalation of their "War on Drugs" into the private sector. (194).

Proponents of drug testing are often guilty of simplistic conclusions that claim causation when there is merely a correlation. Many behaviors of lower-income people often differ statistically from upper-income people, but this mere correlation never establishes causation. It is quite probable, for example, that people who watch Jerry Springer have lower incomes than those who do not. Should we then conclude that television talk shows decrease a worker's productivity? Or, by similar logic, should we conclude that Thunderbird wine hurts productivity but Chivas Regal scotch helps it?

It may be intuitive that drug use is connected to job impairment, but there is no data linking positive drug tests to impairment, intoxication, safety hazards, or decreased work productivity (22-23,1). There has been no established correlation between drug concentration in the blood and behavioral impairment for most drugs except alcohol (24). Only alcohol clearly alters cognitive and motor functions. Thus, a positive drug test does not correlate with any particular pharmacological effect or workplace performance (25). Drugs are often implicated when an accident occurs if they are found to be present in the person involved, but cause is rarely proven (10). A positive drug test also does not indicate how much or when a drug was taken, and it does not indicate the extent of drug use; it may be due to one time use or continual abuse of the drug (12). Even though alcohol is the only drug that clearly alters cognitive and motor functions and is the most frequently abused drug, the Federal Aviation Administration (FAA) announced in January 1998 that it is cutting back on random testing for the presence of alcohol, but will continue to randomly test for other drugs at the same rate (229).

Officials of the U.S. Chamber of Commerce have also testified before Congress and at National Conferences on Drug Abuse that employees who use drugs are "3.6 times more likely to injure themselves or another person in a workplace accident...and five times more likely to file a workers' compensation claim." These numbers are used, and often inflated, to justify drug testing. The drug testing companies often promulgate this information in their "educational" literature. But according to a 1988 article in the *University of Kansas Law Review* by John P. Morgan,

M.D. of the New York City University Medical School, who is an authority on drug testing, the Chamber of Commerce claim is based on a study that has nothing to do with illegal drug users. He traced the claims to an informal study by the Firestone Tire and Rubber Company of employees undergoing treatment for alcoholism (195). Private commercial laboratories performing the bulk of workplace drug testing hawk their services with a vengeance and routinely exaggerate drug abuse statistics to heighten the sense of urgency among prospective clients. One is hard pressed to find marketing material for the drug testing corporations that does not contain grossly exaggerated or made-up statistics. A Psychemedics marketing brochure states, "recent government statistics reveal that 1 out of 6 workers has a drug problem," Another brochure states, "Estimates of on-the-job cocaine use (including crack) range from 10% to 50% of all employees (187)."

In terms of economic costs to society, studies show that a case can be made to test for alcohol abuse, but no logical case can be made for the testing of other drugs (10). Many people feel that drug testing is misguided because alcohol abuse is a much larger problem and accounts for a much greater portion of morbidity in terms of health effects and accidents (4). Despite the fact that alcohol is the most prevalent drug causing work related accidents and that alcohol addiction is much more costly to employers than all illicit drugs combined, the focus is on illicit drugs in the workplace (16). Alcohol contributes to over 100,000 deaths per year and costs society over $100 billion annually in health care, absenteeism, and lost productivity. Furthermore, another legal drug, nicotine, contributes to more than 350,000 deaths per year and costs society $ 60 billion annually in health care, absenteeism, and lost productivity (13).

Also, only alcohol is clearly associated with driving impairment. In 1993, the National Highway Safety Administration concluded in a report to the Department of Transportation: "No clear relationship has ever been demonstrated between marijuana smoking and either seriously impaired driving performance or the risk of accident involvement...There is little if any evidence to indicate that drivers who have used marijuana are any more likely to cause serious accidents than drug free drivers. Drivers under the influence of marijuana retain insight into their performance and will compensate where they can, for example, by slowing down or increasing effort. As a consequence, THC's adverse effects on driving performance appear relatively small (196)." In contrast, studies find a consistent correlation between fatigue and driving performance with performance dropping by 10% after five hours of driving (218). One study that seemed to show that airline pilots had decrements in performance during complex situations 24 hours after smoking marijuana is commonly sited by the drug testing industry. This study was critized, however, for not using proper scientific controls. Its authors conceded that the findings were merely interesting and no real conclusions could be drawn from it (136). In 1997, the National Institute on Drug Abuse examined the effects of marijuana and alcohol on performance of a variety of cognitive and motor tasks. Their results corroberated those of previous studies: alcohol impaired performance but marijuana did not. There is evidence, however, that even though marijuana may not affect stimulus-response reaction time, it can reduce attentiveness (137-139).

Experts in Sweden concluded that, due to individual variation, legal standards could not be set for job impairment due to marijuana (26). "If health, safety, productivity, performance and cost effectiveness are criteria, testing for marijuana should have a very low priority (4)." J. Morland, M.D., Director of the National Institute of Forensic Toxicology in Oslo, Norway, states, "No studies appear to have shown that the infrequent use of alcohol and drugs is risky with regard to workplace performance and productivity...(206)."

The rationale of including prescription medications, such as benzodiazepines, narcotics, and barbiturates, has rarely been challenged even though these medications may be actually improving, rather than hindering an employee's performance. Medication may be taken to treat a person's seizure disorder, anxiety disorder, painful ailments, psychological disorders, or insomnia. Drug testing does not differentiate between those who use medications in a responsible manner from those who abuse drugs (2).

If employers are really concerned about the safety and performance of their employees, they should abandon the ineffective urine testing and measure actual impairment instead. Computer software programs are available that measure hand-eye coordination and response time as compared to the employee's baseline. These arcade like tests can be done quickly and cheaply everyday. It only takes a minute for an employee to complete the test at a desktop computer before working. This would not only detect people who are impaired by drugs and alcohol, but also by sleep depravation, stress, fatigue, emotional problems including anxiety, sickness or other health problems, over-the-counter medications, prescription medications, or are otherwise not able to perform safely.

Impairment due to illicit drugs is statistically much less likely than impairment from other factors. These tests, once administered, can improve safety far better than drug tests can.

Drug testing appears to be another component of the "War on Drugs" that was thought to be a quick and easy fix to a problem that has no quick and easy fixes. As predicted by those knowledgeable about addiction, the "War on Drugs" is a miserable failure. Instead of treating drug addiction as a criminal offense, we need to treat it as the public health problem that it is. Why punish the addict who is already punishing himself more than most can imagine? Making the addict's life more unbearable with jail time, monetary fines, and a criminal record reinforces feelings of hopelessness and keeps the addict from improving his life, which only serves to keep him or her using drugs. Denying an addict employment through drug testing is also a sure way to keep him or her using drugs and alcohol. Furthermore, the addict with no means of support must turn to the streets and obtain money through crime and prostitution or rely on the government for sustenance, which increases drug use in society.

Some claim that drug testing is beneficial because it leads to earlier diagnosis and treatment for drug abuse. This is, unfortunately, not the case because the overwhelming majority of people testing positive are not offered treatment as an option. Instead they are fired with subsequent loss of all unemployment and health benefits. People afflicted with addiction are denied employment, which is their only means of receiving treatment for their disease. Even if it did lead to earlier diagnosis and treatment, should we switch to mandated PAP smears and mammograms? Early detection of cancer could also, perhaps, improve job performance and productivity. Clearly, preemployment drug testing is not in the best interests of employers, employees, addicts, or society as a whole.

Drug testing is a failure in about every measurable end-point as is another government sponsored program, DARE. A federal survey showed teen drug abuse up 78% from 1992 to 1995, and the annual Monitoring the Future survey of 50,000 students in 435 public and private schools showed 1996 to be the fifth consecutive year of increased substance abuse amongst eighth graders (18). In December of 1997, the University of Michigan released its annual Household Survey that shows teens and children continue to use drugs at an earlier age with no significant decrease in drug use. A 1997 survey by the Parents Resource Institute for Drug Education (PRIDE) reported that 11.4% of junior high school students had used drugs the previous month, up from 10.9% during the previous year. There was also no decrease in reported drug use amongst high school students.

Studies show that drug use among kids who have gone through DARE was virtually identical to the level among kids who had not. In 1996, Dick Clayton, M.D., a widely respected drug abuse researcher at the University of Kentucky, published the most rigorous long-term study ever performed on DARE in the *Journal of Preventive Medicine* and published the book *Intervening with Drug-Involved Youth*. He stated, "Although the results from various studies differ somewhat, all studies are consistent in finding that DARE does not have long-term effects on drug use." The studies show that DARE was less effective then anyone imagined. This includes every category of drug use tested, lifetime usage, how often they had used drugs, how recently they had used drugs, and the grade in which they started using drugs. Moreover, students in both groups rated the availability of drugs nearly identical. In fact, the only statistically significant difference between the groups is DARE graduates are more likely to use marijuana and drink alcohol regularly for the purpose of getting drunk. As one researcher stated, "DARE is the world's biggest pet rock. If it makes us feel good to spend the money on nothing, that's okay, but everyone should know DARE does nothing (203)." To refute the negative studies, the directors of DARE also spent millions of dollars to set up their own biased studies that would ensure the results were favorable to DARE, but even these studies showed DARE was no better than doing nothing at keeping kids off drugs.

The simplistic, one sided misinformation, that is the basis of the "Just Say No to Drugs" campaign, undermines legitimate efforts to educate children on the devastating effects of drug abuse. Children quickly realize that the constant simplistic mindless jargon that is the basis of the "Just Say No to Drugs" campaign is not the truth. Subsequently, they disregard any further information presented to them by educators that can help keep them from using drugs. DARE tells children, "No use--No excuse" and to "Just say no" but gives no real reasons why. When addressing a group of Maryland high school students in his 1996 re-election campaign, President Clinton's reason to "Just say no" was, "Drug use is illegal, and therefore it is wrong." I'm sure the students were glad he cleared that up.

The DARE program and the other methods this country employs to deter drug use woefully underestimates both the intelligence and the social skills of young people who use drugs. This shortcoming undermines our ability to communicate important information to our youth about the devastating effects of drug abuse, which if properly executed, could reduce both drug use and the harm associated with its use. Joel Brown, M.D., in his study of California's Drug, Alcohol and Tobacco Education program (DATE), found that by the time kids turned 13 or 14 years old, the overwhelming belief was that educators and police had systematically lied to them about drugs and drug use. This led, Brown concluded, to a general disrespect for authority figures and a disdain for their messages (210).

Our elected leaders should get the message that their simplistic messages don't work. It is ridiculous to believe that by hammering youths with half-truths and drug hysteria messages, there will be any positive effects. It is an insult to the intelligence of our youths. These messages are quickly disregarded as false, and any further information is subsequently ignored. The one sided drug hysteria messages simply pander to the fears of parents and have little basis in either the realities of the lives of teenagers nor do they serve as a pragmatic strategy to actually help kids stay off drugs. Instead, youths should be educated about drugs and their dangers. "In the U.S., the assumption seems to be that we must somehow protect our kids from the facts, lest they be tempted to make choices that make adults uneasy. This strategy has served only to alienate and disenfranchise our youth, leaving them to drift through their world without the very moral compass that our wrongheaded policies are attempting to instill. The lesson to be drawn from these bits of news from among the world is that lies, threats and oppression are likely to lead teens to far different conclusions than the ones we intended for them to reach. So let us reassess our direction (210)."

"In 1988 Congress passed a resolution proclaiming its goal of "a drug-free America by 1995." U.S. drug policy has failed persistently over the decades because it has preferred such rhetoric to reality, and moralism to pragmatism. Politicians confess their youthful indiscretions, then call for tougher drug laws. Drug control officials make assertions with no basis in fact or science. Police officers, generals, politicians, and guardians of public morals qualify as drug czars-but not, to date, a single doctor or public health figure. Independent commissions are appointed to evaluate drug policies, only to see their recommendations ignored as politically risky. And drug policies are designed, implemented, and enforced with virtually no input from the millions of Americans they affect most: drug users. Drug abuse is a serious problem, both for individual citizens and society at large, but the "War on Drugs" has made matters worse, not better (228)."

It is fact that only a small percentage of people who use drugs, including children, will become addicted and suffer any negative consequences from drug use, and the majority of people who have experimented with drugs do so without any ill effects or consequences. A popular DARE message told to children is "Drug use is drug abuse", but contrary to that, they see otherwise. While children and adolescents may know of someone who had a problem with drugs, they know of many others who have used drugs without a problem, especially marijuana. They also see many people who have problems with alcohol but the thought that "alcohol use is alcohol abuse" seems absurd in our alcohol-swilling society. Subsequently the message that "Drug use is drug abuse" is regarded as further evidence that the entire anti-drug message is "a pack of lies". Thus, this type of message, although well intentioned, does more harm than good. Simplistic one sided information rarely works on the complexities of human nature and the human psyche.

A 1997 study out of the United Kingdom, finds that

despite the government-perpetuated stereotypes about what types of kids use drugs, the typical young recreational user is socially well-adjusted, knowledgeable about the substances he or she is using, cognizant how drug use fits into his life, and is strongly disapproving of "out of control" or "problem" use behavior. The report concluded that "most drug use takes place as part of a consumer lifestyle, not a deviant one." The youths were found to be no less moral or more prone to fatalistic thinking than their non-using counterparts (209-210).

In the highly respected, peer reviewed scientific journal, the *American Psychologist* Jonathan Shedler, M.D. and Jack Block, M.D. from the University of California at Berkeley, reported their results form a 15 year investigation of San Francisco area children. Their investigation reveals that adolescents who occasionally use drugs are healthier than both drug abusers and drug abstainers. The adolescents that had engaged in some drug experimentation were the most well-adjusted in the sample. Moreover, those who abused drugs as teen-agers had distinct behavioral problems that were identifiable years before their drug use began. "Problem drug use is a symptom not a cause of personal and social maladjustment," says Dr. Shedler. "Current efforts at drug prevention are misguided to the extent that they focus on symptoms, rather than on the psychological syndrome underlying drug abuse...the most effective drug prevention programs might not deal with drugs at all (220)." This, I believe, is the key to successfully combatting the drug abuse problem in this country. Until we realize that drugs and alcohol are not the problem but merely a symptom, we will continue to fight a losing battle at the expense of our nation's children.

If you look into the reasons why drug abusers, as opposed to occasional recreational users, take drugs, it becomes clear why programs such as drug testing and the DARE program are failing to deter drug use. While many people use drugs and alcohol recreationally without a problem, others use drugs and alcohol to self-medicate and as a solution to inner pain or depression. The latter is much more likely develop an alcohol or drug abuse problem. It is here where our efforts should be concentrated. The drug and alcohol abuser's unhealthy solution will, over time, make his or her pain and depression worse, but it does provide brief periods of relief. Superficial solutions like drug testing and DARE's "Just Say No" program only address a solution used and not the problem. The program does not attempt to deal with the cause of the drug use. People will go to great lengths to avoid emotional pain and suffering, and because using drugs or alcohol is the only way many people know of to escape this inner pain, it is no wonder that programs that don't teach alternative solutions are unsuccessful (see supplement: Addiction). Would a "Just Say No" to depression program reduce the number of people in our country suffering from depression? The recreational user will likely not suffer due to his or her use, but the self-medicators will likely suffer harshly from drug and alcohol abuse or addiction. It may seem impossible to even attempt to separate and treat the drug problem this way, but significant strides will be made if we dispose of the archaic methods of drug hysteria messages and scare tactics and replace them with a more understanding, humanistic approach. This feat can be accomplished by treating drug abuse as the medical condition that it really is.

The DARE program, started in 1983 by the Los Angeles Police Department and the L.A. School District, has many striking similarities with drug testing in this country. As studies began to clearly show that the DARE program and its "Just Say No" strategy wasn't working, it did not become a public issue that a program that costs more than half a billion dollars a year is a waste of taxpayers' money. As with drug testing, the government responded to the overwhelming evidence that the program was ineffective by spending more money, expanding the misguided program and trying to silence any critics of the program. For the past five years, DARE has been known to use tactics ranging from bullying journalists, manipulating studies, intimidating politicians, and stopping news organizations, researchers and parents from criticizing the program. After DARE tried to prevent the *American Journal of Public Health* from publishing a study critical of the DARE program, Sabine Beisler, M.D., editor of the academic journal, stated, "DARE has tried to interfere with the publication of this. They tried to intimidate us." Richard Moran, Ph.D., professor of criminology and sociology at Mount Holyoke University states, What you have to understand is that DARE is almost a billion dollar industry. If you found out that a food company's foods were rotten, they'd be out of business. What's now been found out is that DARE is running the biggest fraud in America. That's why they've gone nuts. DARE has become so well known for the hardball tactics it employs to shut down its critics that drug researchers and journalists have a word for those hushed--they say they've been 'dared' (203)." Ralph Lochridge, a spokesman for DARE, denied that DARE tried to silence researchers and journalists. He said, "It does try to help journalists write balanced pieces." It's impossible to say exactly how many researchers have been "dared", but it is common knowledge that doing

DARE studies can ruin a promising career.

The ineffective DARE program is now being dropped in a few cities across the country. But support for DARE, as with drug testing, continues despite, at best, disappointing results. No one, not parents, not educators, not researchers, and certainly not DARE officials, want to hear the bad news that it is useless. Politicians have found support of DARE and drug testing to be vital to a successful political career because the public has been shielded from the facts. Current laws actually prevent substance abuse funds from being distributed to programs that stray away from the "Just Say No" message. Unable to produce any data that refutes DARE's ineffectiveness, an Indiana DARE official's justification for the ineffective program became: "If they could just see the kids' faces, they'd know how much good it's doing."

We will never truly know the devastating effects that ineffective methods of combatting the drug abuse problems such as drug testing and DARE have had and continues to have on American and our children. It has not only taken away funding for programs that have shown to be successful in treating drug, but it has also served to harness the continued ignorance that drug abuse can be stomped out. Likewise, drug testing is also fostering this punitive mentality toward drug abuse that is proven to be an ineffective strategy at deterring drug use. The sooner we realize the truth and abandon reactionary efforts, the sooner we can move on to successfully treating the drug abuse problem in this country.

A major Kingpin for the drug testing industry and the "War on Drugs" has been Congressman Gerald Solomon, Chairman of the powerful House Rules Committee. He has introduced proposals into Congress that would make refusal to submit to arbitrary drug testing a federal violation for which one would be summarily declared as having tested positive. He has also submitted proposals in the first session of the 105th Congress that would: deny federal education benefits for those convicted of any drug offense (HR 88); implement pre-employment drug testing of all federal job applicants (HR89); implement random drug testing for many non-safety sensitive federal employees (HR 90,92,310); prohibit the use of federal funds for drug legalization issues (HR 313); eliminate court discretion in connection with denial of various federal benefits for those convicted of drug offenses (HR 313); require that courts notify employers of employee drug offense convictions (HR333); and mandate that states lose federal highway funds if they don't enact a law that suspends the driver's license of anyone convicted of a drug offense (Solomon-Lautenberg Amendment), which was specifically intended to punish marijuana consumers in the states in which marijuana possession for personal use only carries a small fine (187).

Soloman is aggressively pursuing a cultural war against certain lifestyles and modes of social and political thought. He is noted for his speech on the House floor following the ground offensive against Iraq where he stated, "What we cannot be proud of is the unshaven, shaggy-haired, drug culture, poor excuses for Americans, wearing their tiny round wire-rim glasses, a protester's symbol of the blame-America-first crowd, out in front of the White House burning the American Flag (188)." Soloman is also for legislation outlawing the use of the internet to disseminate and discuss drug legalization information, and for denying tax-exempt status to non-profit organizations "favoring drug legalization," with retroactive taxing of those found to be sympathetic to such organizations (189). All this from a man who on October 7, 1994 stated in a House of Representatives debate, "Today is the beginning of the second Reagan Revolution that will shrink the size and power of the federal government. No longer will there be an arrogant attitude around here that says Big Brother Federal Government knows best (190)."

The following are a few government proposals that will dramatically increase the use of drug testing in this country. Along with this increase there will, undoubtedly, be growing numbers of people who will suffer when they are falsely labeled drug users by the inaccuracies of drug testing. People will unjustly be denied a driver's license, evicted from their homes, and be denied their rights to government benefits.

A Federal Register announcement earlier this summer asked states to submit proposals for funding to develop plans to test all teenagers applying for licenses, and anyone involved in an accident or cited for a traffic violation. If this were to become national policy it would expand the preemployment drug testing dragnet by tens of millions a year (62 Fed. Reg. 35887-35892,July 2, 1997).

Newt Gingrich continued his "War on Drugs" political grandstanding with an appearance on a news conference to announce the introduction of a legislative proposal that requires drug tests of all U.S. newborns, despite being adamantly opposed by the majority of health care officials including the American Academy of Pediatrics (187). On the welfare front, the federal welfare reform legislation of 1996 authorizes states to drug test recipients of aid by stating: "States shall not be prohibited by the federal government from testing welfare recipients for use of controlled substances nor from sanctioning welfare recipients who test positive for use of controlled substances." Already ten states have passed laws authorizing drug testing in some form. Once again the poor and defenseless are made weaker by the drug war. Oregon passed a strange law this year that allows landlords to demand a urine sample from tenants. If the tenants test positive, the landlord is allowed to evict the tenant (1997 Or. S.B. 675, 69th Leg. Assembly). Louisiana has gone the furthest of any state by passing a law that requires random, suspicionless and mandatory drug testing of anyone who receives anything of economic value from the state. A positive test results in mandatory drug treatment, which is paid for by the individual's insurance or the individual. Refusal to take a test, or a second positive test results in a loss of any economic benefit from the state, e.g., termination, removal, loss of license, loan, scholarship, contract or public assistance (1997 L.A. H.B. 2435,1997).

In Bangkok, Thailand, hundreds of night-clubbers have been rounded up in midnight raids and forced to undergo drug tests. While this may seem extreme and unlikely to happen here in the United States because it would be considered a Constitutional Rights violation, all that is needed is for the courts to deem patrons of night clubs to be at high risk for drug use and rule there is a "special need" to control drug use in this group. This would justify any infringing upon their civil rights. As drug testing proves to be ineffective at combatting the drug abuse problem in this country, the government continues its typical reactionary reasoning that drug testing is unsuccessful because not enough people are being tested. Thus, drug testing will continue to expand and invade many aspects of our lives. Unless this country realizes that drug abuse can not be extinguished by force, such "rounding-up" and ferreting out of "high risk" individuals may, unfortunately, not be far off.

Employment drug testing, which began as a well-intentioned, although reactionary, idea to help curb the drug abuse problem in this country, is a proven failure. It has been promulgated by lies and deceit for financial gain of the powerful drug testing industry and by government officials wanting to appear active in the fight against drugs on our home front. Many people realize that drug testing may be devastating the lives of some but feel that something must be done to curtail this nation's drug use; they feel the end justifies the means. But drug testing is merely a figurative offering of hope. It is not decreasing drug abuse. It is not making for a safer workplace. It does

47

not encourage rehabilitation. It is not cost-beneficial for employers. And, as discussed in the following chapters, it is being used to unfairly discriminate, and it is devastating the lives of the people it was designed to protect. It is my sincere hope that the information provided to you in this book will allow you to see through the deception that is the basis of the drug testing juggernaut.

What Your Employer May Know About You

Testing for recreational drug use is unlikely to be cost effective for employers unless additional information is obtained that is financially beneficial to the employer (1). Finding that an applicant has a medical condition that requires medication is considered to be valuable information that does make a drug testing program cost effective (19). An employer can easily, without an employee or applicant's knowledge, find out what medications he or she is taking simply by requesting a complete medication screen (2). Employers may then base their hiring decision, in part, on what medication the job candidate is taking. This is a common practice and rarely arouses a laboratory's suspicion. The laboratories are eager for business and usually maintain a "no questions asked" policy. In short, companies are eliminating job candidates and forcing employees out of jobs based upon illegally obtained confidential medical information (19).

By using drug testing, employers are learning what medications employees and applicants are using and screening out "less desirable" candidates, which includes those individuals that are likely to need sick leave or use medical benefits. Thus, anybody being treated for depression, anxiety, heart disease, ulcers, insomnia, diabetes, or high blood pressure may be "screened out" and denied employment as a result of drug testing. A business owner who admitted to screening prospective employees for antidepressants stated, "I do have some reservations about screening for prescription medications, but I'm a businessman. I need to stay competitive. I can't afford to spend the money to train someone then have them go off on a bout of depression. I'm just protecting myself." American Bio Medica, a major drug test manufacturer, is capitalizing on this desire to "weed-out" applicants with any mental health problems. Their newest on-site drug detection assay, the Rapid Drug Screen, not only screens for illicit drugs, but it specifically screens for antidepressants as well. This allows employers to avoid hiring applicants being treated for depression quickly and easily.

Employers have also found it very cost effective to screen female candidates for pregnancy. All this is easily done without the applicant's knowledge (19). This is commonly done by employers that do their own on-site testing. Even the Washington D.C. police department has admitted that it routinely subjected urine specimens taken for drug tests from female police officers and other female employees to pregnancy testing without the employees knowledge or consent (211).

Employers have learned that they don't need to pay the extra money to screen for all medications. They can learn what medications an employee or prospective employee is taking when they receive the list of medications taken in the last 3 months that is submitted before taking the drug test (2). For obvious reasons, employers do not tell applicants that because of their prescription medication use, the job was given to someone else. Job candidates are given other reasons to why they didn't get the job (27). They are never told that employment was denied because they are being treated for heart disease, depression, high blood pressure, or anxiety.

Even if an employer doesn't intentionally find out what medications an employee is taking, drug testing invariably allows confidential medical information to become known to others in the workplace. Confidentiality of drug test results is very difficult to ensure. Despite safeguards and precautions to ensure privacy, prescribed medications inevitably surface and become known to others throughout the company (2,19). There are countless ways in which supposedly confidential results become common knowledge amongst company employees. Because of the large number of people with access to an employee's test results and to the list of medications submitted by the employee prior to taking a drug test, the chance of information leaking out to others is high. Also, once an employee tests positive, the additional administrative procedures he or she must undergo alerts others to the results of the drug test (2). I have yet to see a positive drug test remain confidential. Not only do positive results quickly become known to others in the company, but also the government and insurance companies are notified to deny all possible benefits to those who test positive. A person testing positive will find it difficult to obtain future employment because perspective employers will be told of the positive drug test when they contact the former employer for a reference. Information from drug tests is also being shared via computer data bases with other employers, government agencies, and insurance companies. It has turned into high-tech blacklisting. I know of many people who have tested positive due to laboratory error and have been essentially blackballed from working in their home towns. In addition, employment drug tests results are now being used in court and can be received as evidence, obtained in discovery, and disclosed in any civil or administrative proceeding.

People who are aware that their prescription medication will be revealed to their employer are not applying for jobs with companies doing drug testing, or they are abstaining from using necessary medications. If drug tested, there is a good chance that a person's medical treatment will become known to the employer and adversely effect one's career. Employers are routinely using drug tests to interfere with employees' medical treatment and oftentimes will question the choice of medications prescribed by the employees' physicians (19). With the high rate of mental health problems that require psychoactive medications, many people are being discriminated against, having their medical confidentiality breached, and their civil rights violated (2). From a societal perspective, workplace testing to detect medical conditions or medically approved prescription drug use should be particularly objectionable. The older population, who are more likely to use medication, and those people with psychiatric disorders such as depression are very vulnerable to discrimination, and drug testing allows for a quick and easy way for employers to illegally discriminate against this group of people. These repercussions are a heavy price to pay for the small and questionable benefits of employment drug testing.

Drug Testing: The Essence of Inaccuracy

Drug testing laboratories and those who make public drug policy are reluctant to admit to the weaknesses of drug testing. These powers have purposely withheld any information that would have a negative impact on the current push for widespread drug testing. Drug testing has become a billion dollar business, and clinical laboratories are looking to drug testing as a way to expand their laboratory services to enhance revenue (29). Being significantly different from clinical testing, laboratories that were never intended or designed for the purpose of testing for illicit drugs are being overwhelmed with the demands required of drug testing. Mistakes and errors have been cropping up with alarming frequency. In a 1996 edition of *The Lancet,* John W. Honour, M.D. writes, "Recent examples of grave injustices resulting from flawed scientific and forensic evidence brings into question the drug testing procedures. A false-positive result...can have a cruel impact on the life of anyone found guilty, and there may be no right of appeal (28)."

Unlike clinical laboratory testing, where results are used for the management of patients, non-clinical substance abuse testing is used for punitive ends such as dismissal or denial of employment. Moreover, clinical results have the benefit of review by a physician who looks at the laboratory values in relation to the entire patient, whereas, drug testing results stand on their own merit, often without the benefit of review by anyone prior to being released to the employer (24). Thus, a drug testing laboratory should produce scientific and legally defensible results, which is unfamiliar to clinical laboratories (24). "David Greenblatt, M.D. and Richard Shader, M.D., Editors-in-Chief of the *Journal of Psycho-pharmacology* write, "A positive result may have grave consequences for an individual's job and freedom (5-8). Any nonzero false positive rate, no matter how low, inflicts unnecessary suffering upon society and should not be tolerated, particularly when there is no clinical indication for a test in the first place (3)."

Clinical laboratories are not experienced with the special requirements for specimen collection, analysis, storage, documentation, transport, and handling (10,24). Clinical laboratories are trying to perform the additional burdens required of drug testing without additional expenditures that assure quality testing. They are notorious for generating false positive results by mislabeling specimens (someone else's urine being labeled as yours), contamination crossover (glassware used to transfer the urine to and from the testing apparatus is contaminated by previous drug containing urine samples), and from instrumental, technician and reporting errors, (10,29,216). The contamination of glassware with positive urine alone has been shown to cause a 3 to 5 percent false positive rate (173).

The general public erroneously believes that drug testing is accurate and reliable. Because drug testing has become a very competitive industry, laboratories are implementing cost cutting measures and attempting to test increasing numbers of specimens quicker and cheaper, which is causing testing accuracy to worsen even further (10,29-30). Robert Gladd, laboratory certified quality engineer, states, "My own long and intense laboratory tenure indelibly persuaded me of what any honest lab manager will admit: analytical quality is a principal casualty of specimen overload (187)." Courts have ruled that drug testing techniques must have only general scientific acceptance (31). They are not required to have absolute accuracy (32).

Any laboratory, regardless of how poor its testing methods, may contract with employers to do drug testing. Drug testing price quotes range from $10 to $490 per employee tested (30). Because the employer or testing authority usually isn't familiar with the complexities of drug testing and data on laboratory testing accuracy is unavailable, the drug testing contract is usually granted to the lowest bidding laboratory even though it may utilize inferior testing methods that generate inaccurate results. Only federal employees and those from the private sector being tested under federal mandate, such as those involved with public transportation, are required to utilize laboratories that are certified by the National Institute on Drug Abuse and follow guidelines set up in 1988 by the U.S. Department of Health and Human Services. These guidelines are not applicable to laboratories testing employees in the private sector. Thus, the large majority of people are tested by laboratories that do not follow any guidelines. In a six state survey in the mid-South, only 24% of private testing laboratories used the federal guidelines for drug concentration cutoff level, which is designed to limit false positive results (36). Cutoff levels for both the immunoassays and GC-MS have been arbitrarily changed and often vary within and between laboratories (226). Increasing numbers of employers are also doing their own on-site drug screening without following any guidelines. These on-site testing methods comprised about 15 percent of the tests done in 1987, and with the recent aggressive marketing of these devices, they are now commonplace (181). The employers are free to test for any substance they choose and perform the tests in any manner they wish (37). The accuracy of these methods is shown to be even worse than those done in certified laboratories (182-186). Of the initial 100 laboratories that applied for certification by the NIDA, only 50 were able to achieve sufficiently high accuracy and perform proper testing procedures to become certified (The NIDA would not release further information) (1). However, the inability to pass certification requirements in no way limits a laboratory's testing ability because certification is not needed to do drug testing.

The many problems of drug testing have been withheld by the laboratories and governmental agencies and overlooked by the media. In fact, only 85 of the estimated 1,200 laboratories in the United States meet federal standards for accuracy, qualified lab personnel, and proper documentation and record-keeping (223). In 1989, a study by the National Institute of Drug Abuse (NIDA) on drug testing proficiency showed that of the 73 laboratories reporting their results of the tested samples, only 8 laboratories reported the results correctly (correctly means that a sample that contained a drug tested positive and a sample that contained no drug tested negative). The NIDA attempted to keep the results from becoming public, and it has taken 6 years of legal action to force the NIDA to divulge some of the results (33). Still only limited information about the results is available because the NIDA obliterated much of the data that would have been most damaging to the drug testing industry (30).

The Center for Disease Control (CDC) evaluated the performance of 13 laboratories that analyzed samples for methadone treatment facilities (177). Samples with known quantities of barbiturates, amphetamines, methadone, cocaine, codeine, and morphine were prepared and submitted blind (the laboratories thought they were patient samples). The laboratorys' performance varied widely: error rates of 0 to 94 percent in false negatives (labs unable to detect drugs present in the samples) and 0 to 66 percent false positive errors (drugs detected by the labs were not in the samples). Commenting on the CDC study, David Smith, M.D., director of the Haight Ashbury Free

Clinic said, "in many cases the labs would have done a better job if they had poured the urine down the drain and flipped a coin. (173)." In defense of the poor results, Bob Fogerson, quality assurance manager at the drug testing firm Pharm Chem, argued that "it is not valid to conclude drug testing can not be done accurately just because we have not been doing it a accurately."

The accuracy of drug testing laboratories, if ever publicized, is always grossly inflated (24). Because true accuracy results would be damaging to a laboratory's reputation, laboratories will either regurgitate the accuracy promoted by the manufacturers of the testing apparatus or refer to the accuracy of the analysis by expert technicians on known control samples made from sterilized synthetic urine. The quoted rates are valid only for the analysis of known control samples consisting of one pure substance in sterile urine or water that is free from interfering substances being tested under ideal conditions by expert technicians without time or cost constraints. In the real world, specimens are from average people who ingest a variety of foods, additives, over-the-counter preparations, and prescription medicines; and these specimens are tested by technicians with varying skill levels under both time and cost restraints (34). In 1995, a study by the University of Health Center published in the medical journal *Drug and Alcohol Dependence* compared the accuracy of drug tests performed by expert laboratory personnel with drug tests performed by the personnel who would normally be performing the analysis on routine samples. They found that when the highly trained personnel performed the tests, the tests were extremely accurate. But when the tests were performed by the those who would actually be testing routine samples under normal working conditions, the accuracy rate dropped to 82%. The authors of the study state that the drug testing products need to "be evaluated under normal working conditions with the personnel who will be required to perform routine testing (224)." Drug testing manufacturers always evaluate the accuracy of their products when used by expert technicians under ideal conditions, making the results meaningless for real-life situations.

The Einsel commission, an investigative commission of the Department of Defense, released a report in March 1984 showing an alarming false positive rate at the military labs: Forts Mead (97% false positive rate (FPR)), Brooks (60% FPR), Wiesbaden (75% FPR), and at Trippler (20% FPR). It is argued that the newer testing devices are now more accurate and less prone to false positives. But according to the Einsel commission report, most errors were related to human error. The bulk of the errors could be attributed to inadequate personnel, poor management, broken chain of custody, faulty maintenance, and faulty transmissions of reports and records, rather than the tests themselves. Testing devices are more accurate, on average, than those used when the study was done in 1984, but the average laboratory worker is less educated and receives less training than they did in 1984. Because drug tests are only as good as those performing the tests, the advancements in the technology have failed to significantly improve the accuracy rates. False positives continue to occur at unacceptable rates.

Daniel Buer, M.D., Chief of Laboratory Services of the Veterans Administration Medical Center in Portland Oregon, agrees that untrained staff is a significant cause of false positive drug tests regardless of the technology. He and others (181-186) have found that test results produced by individuals with limited laboratory training are less reliable. He states, "Analysts with limited training...are generally not aware of the quality management practices necessary to maintain the technical reliability of the results they produce. Because of their limited training it is also likely that they are unaware of test specificity problems which cause a significant fraction of positive results to be falsely positive (181)." The European scientific community is well aware of how inadequately trained personnel are causing enormous problems with false positive results in the United States. J. Morland, M.D., Director of the National Institute of Forensic Toxicology in Oslo, Norway writes in his critical review of drug testing in the United States, "In summary, the highest skill levels are required by (a) the medical personnel collecting the information and the sample; (b) the analytical laboratory; and (c) the medical review officer interpreting the results for the employer. At those three stages-sample collection, sample analysis and interpretation of results-serious mistakes can be made if the personnel involved lack the necessary competence or instruments. Such mistakes can easily lead to wrong results and eventually, the punishment of innocent employees (206)." At a recent laboratory sciences conference with over 120 forensic laboratory scientists and drug testing experts, many who work for manufacturers of drug tests, a question was asked, "Is there anybody who would submit urine for drug testing if his career, reputation, freedom or livelihood depended upon it?" Not a single hand was raised (211). David Smith, M.D. pointed out at a California State Senate Hearing to evaluate the need for lab regulations that "in mass testing, without probable cause, error is inevitable." Smith points out that typically the cheapest tests are used, employers are rarely told the limitations or the true accuracy rates of the tests, and often the lab technicians themselves do not understand the testing process or how the data needs to be interpreted (173).

In 1995, Beverly A. Potter, Ph.D. investigated the accuracy claims of the drug testing manufacturers. She states, "Manufacturers of drug tests say that their instruments are 95 to 99 percent accurate at detecting traces of drugs in urine, when their own lab employees operate the machines while closely watched for proficiency. Manufacturers claim that the gas chromatography/mass spectrometer is nearly 100 percent accurate. But these high accuracy rates hold only when the lab operators are extremely proficient and diligent. Such ideal conditions virtually never exist in practice. Commercial drug test manufacturers sell and lease their instruments to private labs and hospitals. There is no government or industry agency responsible for monitoring the quality of work done at these labs. The reality is that the machines are only as reliable as the people operating them. Careless, overworked, or incompetent operators can misuse the machines in innumerable ways, yielding false positive results on clean urine specimens."

Actual advertisement from a 1998 *Entrepreneur* magazine to become a Substance Abuse Testing Professional with no previous medical education or experience required.

Because drug testing laboratories are competing for contracts from employers, the testing contract is usually granted to the lowest bidding laboratory. Thus, there is significant pressure on laboratories to limit costs. To remain competitive, laboratories have increased the numbers and speed of testing while decreasing the cost of performing the tests by utilizing less educated and improperly trained personnel and by eliminating costly quality assurance programs, including proficiency testing, which was designed to decrease the numbers of false positives. The actual tests may be more accurate when compared to a decade ago, but cost cutting measures have resulted in the production of an alarming number of false positive results. Accurate and reliable results are simply too expensive. Also, as drug testing is expanded to include larger groups that have a low prevalence of drug use, the percentages of false positives will constitute a larger percentage of all positive results (212-213).

The Substance-Abuse Testing Committee of the American Association for Clinical Chemistry also noted false positive results caused by the use of inferior reference control samples. They noted problems of control sample purity and the improper use of synthetic control samples to measure the sensitivity, specificity, and quality control parameters of the drug testing apparatus. They felt it was improper to infer that the control samples have the same properties as natural urine samples with numerous biological components. Drugs behave differently when analyzed in a specimen derived from the body after administration than they do when added to sterilized urine (28). Thus, a biological positive control sample (a urine sample from a person who has ingested the drug in question) should be used as a reference standard for proper interpretation of a test result. But because artificial control samples are less expensive to prepare, they are used almost exclusively as reference standards, resulting in testing errors (28). In short, the control samples do not resemble the urine specimens as is needed for accurate analysis. The Substance-Abuse Testing Committee also noted that the problem is compounded because false positive results (testing positive for drugs when no drugs are actually present) generated in this manner are not revealed using the current approach of analyzing replicate samples (24).

In addition, accuracy testing is usually performed by submitting known control samples (samples that the laboratory testing personnel know are for accuracy testing). Laboratories, however, perform much better on the known control samples than on samples submitted "blindly" (unknown to testing personnel) for routine analysis (24). A series of studies by the Centers for Disease Control (CDC) showed that laboratories performed significantly better on known control samples than on samples thought to be routine (35). In all the studies, the number of false positive and false negative results increased greatly when accuracy testing samples were submitted as routine samples, as compared with the same samples being submitted as known control samples. Thus, a laboratory's performance on accuracy tests represents the laboratory's best effort and does not indicate the true ability to process and analyze routine samples (10). Laboratories were able to correctly determine if one of six drugs was present in known control samples 95% of the time, but if the specimens were submitted "blind", meaning that the laboratory did not know that they were test samples, the laboratories were able to correctly determine if one of the six drugs were present only 46.5% of the time (10). Even blind proficiency testing does not evaluate a laboratory's ability to accurately analyze routine samples because no potential cross-reacting substances are permitted in the performance samples. The proficiency guidelines state that for the blind performance specimens, "The positive samples shall be spiked only with those drugs for which the agency is testing." The guidelines have been set up by the drug testing industry to protect itself because few labs would accurately analyze the proficiency samples if they also contained cross-reacting metabolites from over-the-counter and prescription medications as is the case in real-life.

Arthur J. McBay Ph.D., Chief Medical Examiner of the Departments of Pathology and Pharmacology at the University of North Carolina and Chief Medical Examiner for the State of North Carolina, writes, "There have been reports of proficiency testing for private enterprises, but unfortunately the results have not generally been available to independent experts in adversarial proceedings. When private laboratory personnel have been asked about the accuracy of their tests, they have responded that their work is 95% or 99% accurate. Rather than offering documentation to support their claim, they may cite the manufacturer's pamphlet describing testing performed on drug-supplemented specimens or some scientific paper published on testing similar to their method, but they offer no evidence of the quality of their own work (10). Laboratories are reporting the identification and quantitation of drugs at concentrations lower than those for which they have demonstrate capability of identifying and quantitating. The private employer is not required to obtain a confirmatory test or to use a certified laboratory. At the present time, I know of no laboratory doing workplace drug testing that I could confidently recommend for urine or blood testing...(215)"

Alerted by the increasing numbers of non-drug users being labeled as drug users, the President of The American Association for Clinical Chemistry formed a Substance Abuse Testing Committee to analyze the problems of drug testing. The committee felt that to decrease the increasing numbers of false positive results, laboratories must exhibit significantly "higher quality assurance than is currently in place for clinical laboratories," and they must recognize and "accept the considerable costs necessary for quality assurance (24)." The committee felt that drastic measures must be taken and that each laboratory should hire a Laboratory Certifying Scientist (LCS) whose job it would be to ensure that results are obtained according to established quality-assurance criteria. Laboratories have rejected the recommendations arguing that the additional costs to assure quality and accuracy would put them out of business. Thus, there are virtually no safeguards against false positive results, and laboratories continue to run amok (24).

Because there are no set guidelines for the majority of drug testing laboratories, there is no set technique for analyzing drugs of abuse. A person's urine may be tested using a variety of immunoassays and chromatographic techniques.

Immunoassays

Immunoassays are the most often used testing method for drugs of abuse because they can be purchased and maintained inexpensively. They use an antibody that recognizes a certain chemical structure of the drug in question. The antibodies are placed in the urine specimen along with an enzyme that is permanently attached to the drug that the assay is designed to analyze. If no drugs are in the urine, the antibody is free to bind with the drug-enzyme complex, which inactivates the enzyme. Thus, when substrate (a substance transformed by the enzyme) is subsequently added, no reaction takes place (See figure 1).

If a drug is present in the urine, the antibodies bind to it instead of the drug-enzyme complex, and the enzyme is not inactivated. Thus, when substrate is subsequently added, it is transformed into a product that changes the absorption of light passing through the solution, signaling a positive test (See figure 1).

Figure 1

Detection of drugs using immunoassay

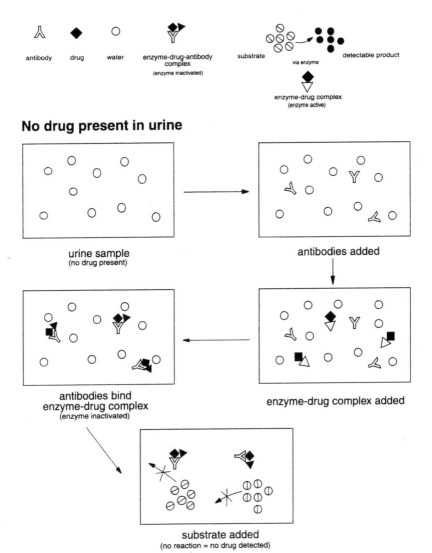

No drug present in urine

urine sample
(no drug present)

antibodies added

antibodies bind
enzyme-drug complex
(enzyme inactivated)

enzyme-drug complex added

substrate added
(no reaction = no drug detected)

Drug present in urine

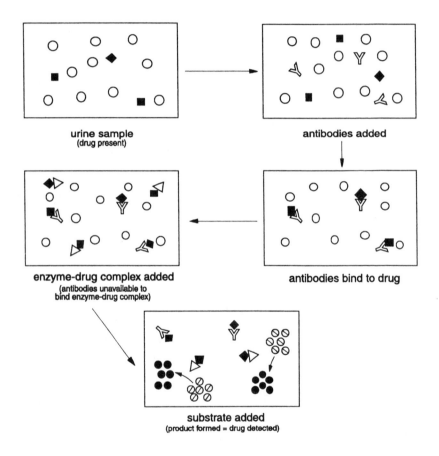

urine sample
(drug present)

antibodies added

enzyme-drug complex added
(antibodies unavailable to
bind enzyme-drug complex)

antibodies bind to drug

substrate added
(product formed = drug detected)

Because the antibody recognizes structures, the immunoassays can cross react with structurally similar drugs and sometimes unrelated compounds (38-41). When the antibody cross reacts with other compounds, the assay reads that there is a drug in the urine when there is not. This is known as a false positive reading.

There are three basic types of immunoassays: radioimmunoassay (RIA, Roche), enzyme immunoassay (EMIT, Syva), and fluorescence polarization immunoassay (FPIA, Abbott/TDx). These use different indicators for signaling a positive test. The RIA uses a radiolabeled derivative of the drug being tested, EMIT uses an enzyme product as an indicator, and the FPIA uses fluorescence as an indicator (64). The enzyme immunoassay is the most common.

There are also numerous brands of immunoassays made by different manufacturers with varying degrees of reliability, accuracy, and precision (42-46). Regardless of the technology used, numerous reports of false-positive results (showing that drugs are in the urine sample when they are not) have appeared (47-50). The false positive rate has been shown to vary widely from 0.8 to 60%. Thus, at some laboratories, over half the people testing positive will not have any drugs in their urine. Because the consequences of a positive drug test are so severe, only the highest forensic standards should be acceptable. It appears, however, that society is willing to accept a significant number of people being falsely labeled as drug abusers.

Despite having a 4-34% false positive rate (42-43,46,51), the EMIT has been the most widely used immunological assay for detection of drugs of abuse in urine (52). After testing the accuracy of the EMIT immunoassay, Michael Hailer, Ph.D. et al, from the Department of Toxicology at the Institute of Forensic Medicine University of Munich, assessed the study results and stated, "This fits quite well with the examinations of other authors, who have already shown that...this assay is subject to various uncontrollable external influences that can evoke such remarkable deviation that it makes it very difficult to obtain correctly reproducible test results (52)."

The TRIAGE immunoassay was introduced in 1994 for drug testing (53). It is also widely used: 42% of the 2200 participants in the 1995 American Association for Clinical Chemistry and College of American Pathologist Urine Drug Testing Survey use the TRIAGE immunoassay (54). It was shown that this widely used assay can routinely produce over 50% false positive results for amphetamines, barbiturates, and cocaine on drug free urine (43,53).

One study cited is a comprehensive investigation comparing the accuracy of the most common drug testing devices entitled "Drugs-of-Abuse Testing in Urine: Statistical Approach and Experimental Comparison of Immunochemical and Chromatographic Techniques" in the *Medical Journal of Analytical Toxicology*. One part of this study compared the positive predictive values of differing commercial brands of the most common method of drug testing. The positive predictive value is the likelihood that a positive test is actually due to a person taking the drug tested. For instance, positive predictive value of 90 would mean that 9 out of 10 people testing positive actually used the drug and 1 out of 10 was due to apparatus error. Below is a portion of the results.

Positive Predictive Value of Common
Drug Testing Devices

Values indicate the likelihood that a person testing positive
for amphetamines with the most common drug testing
devices was actually due to amphetamine use

Technique	Positive for Amphetamines
EMIT-1	82.9
EMIT-2	92.0
ADx	90.1
RIA	94.1
ONTRAK	49.9
EZ-SCREEN	22.5
Triage	55.5
Toxi-Lab	92.2
REMEDI	68.5
HPLC	93.9

These results show that for 100 people testing positive on
a drug screen for amphetamines, between 6 and 78 people
will falsely be labeled a drug user depending upon the
apparatus used.

To improve detection, urine metabolites (by-products of
human metabolism) are often processed with enzymes
called beta-glucurnidases (55-56). The beta
glucuronidases are obtained from shell fish, bacteria, pigs,
and limpets (57). There have been frequent problems with

the enzymatic purity; some of the beta-glucuronidases are contaminated with other enzymes, such as sulfatase and acid phosphatase, that form cross reacting substances and produce false positive results (58). Laboratories are also known to modify the analyzers to use inferior in-house and diluted reagents as cost saving measures, which have been shown by many studies to cause analysis errors (59-60,198-202).

Chromatography

The other commonly used testing method is chromatography, which is performed on a glass plate coated with silica gel. The urine sample is first processed to extract by a variety of methods and then concentrated. This concentrate is spotted across the lower portion of the plate, and the plate is placed upright in an organic solvent. The solvent mixture migrates upward carrying with it the various substances in the urine. Compounds with differing structures will migrate upward to different positions on the plate. The sample is then dried and sprayed with a reagent that is designed to react with the drugs in question to produce a characteristic color. The test is considered positive if there is a spot and it is judged to be of characteristic color and location on the glass (61). To extract higher amounts of drugs from urine while economizing on reagents, many solvent concoctions are used, and accuracy has been shown to vary with different reagent formulations and dilutions (44,62). Some solvent concoctions are shown to complicate the chromatogram with interfering substances making interpretation difficult and causing false positive results (63). The certainty of chromatography depends upon the ability of the technician performing the assays and on the ability of those making the identification. "Most urines contain substances that produce spots on thin-layer chromatograms so as to mask or be misinterpreted as the analyte being sought (10)."

Gas chromatography-mass spectrometry

Because analysis by immunoassay and chromatography frequently give false positive results, federal guidelines set by the National Institute on Drug Abuse (NIDA) require that specimens found positive by the immunoassay be confirmed positive by a gas chromatograph-mass spectrometer (GC-MS). As mentioned earlier, these guidelines need only be followed by laboratories testing employees who are connected with the federal government. Only 4 states, Louisiana, Minnesota, Vermont, and Rhode Island, have attempted to decrease the numbers of false positives by requiring positive tests be confirmed by the GC-MS. Laboratories have lobbied against such regulation citing the fact that the expense of such a requirement would put many smaller laboratories out of business. Most drug testing laboratories do not use or even have access to the prohibitively expensive gas chromatograph-mass spectrometer (24).

Before being analyzed by the gas chromatograph-mass spectrometer, the specimen must first be hydrolyzed, concentrated, and processed to extract. The concentrated extract is heated to a gas and passed through a column coated with a special material that attracts the different molecules to varying degrees depending upon the molecule's polarity (the distribution of electrical charges) and weight, and other molecular attractions. The different types of molecules emerge from the tube at different times depending upon the attraction between the molecules and the substance lining the column walls. Thus, the different types of molecules are separated (64). As the compounds emerge from the gas chromatograph, they are then sent into the mass spectrometer. Here the compounds are bombarded by high energy electrons, causing each compound to fragment. The fragmentation pattern (mass spectrum) is unique and reproducible for every compound so the resulting fragmentation patterns are compared to known standards and identified. Thus, GC-MS can be used to identify any drug or medication requested (64).

The gas chromatograph-mass spectrometer is more accurate when operated by expert technicians than either an immunoassay or chromatography, but because it is expensive to use, most uncertified laboratories will not use it (24). Also, operation of the GC-MS and the interpretation of mass spectral data require a high level of skill, experience, and expertise to produce accurate results. So even if the GC-MS is used, it is usually operated by staff and technicians that lack the appropriated training, which often results in both false negative and false positive results (66-69,181,206,217). Also, when the GC-MS is used it is usually operated in a selected ion monitoring mode which saves money and allows the detection of much smaller amounts of drug by only monitoring one part of the mass spectrum. However, many compounds look identical when only one portion of the spectra is monitored, leading to high rates of false positive results. Laboratories will always grossly inflate the accuracy of the mass spectrometer. They quote the accuracy as if it is run in the full-ion mode, which is rarely the case. The accuracy is considerably less when it is in the selected-ion mode and very prone to false positive results. The accuracy of the GC-MS, as it is used in the majority of testing laboratories, does not approach the accuracy claims made by the drug testing industry (34,65,216,230).

Lorna T. Sniegoski, Ph.D. and Michael J. Welch, Ph.D., from the Analytical Chemistry Division of the Chemical Science and Technology Laboratory at the National Institute of Standards and Technology, compared drug testing laboratories that use the gas chromatograph-mass spectrometer and found human error by "non-expert" technicians caused a significant number of false positive results with the GC-MS. They write, "Of the laboratories using GC-MS, some produced consistently good results, whereas others produced results of poorer quality (66)." In fact, when they were operated by under-qualified technicians, as is often the case, over-the-counter medications like ephedrine and pseudophed were sometimes converted to methamphetamine, rendering people's urine full of illicit drugs after using these over-the-counter cold preparations (67-68,217). Methamphetamine in concentrations of over 4500 ng/ml (9 times the cutoff limit) have been shown to be produced in this manner (69). Dirty injection ports have also caused false positive results (67).

In response to the large numbers of false positive results being generated by gas chromatograph-mass spectrometers, the director of Applied Research for the National Institute on Drug Abuse sent a letter to all certified laboratories stating that a positive test must undergo a second GC-MS confirmation test in which the urine is chemically treated in a different manner than the first confirmatory GC-MS test (68). However, because a second analysis by a GC-MS is expensive, it is rarely done even by certified laboratories. The GC-MS is, obviously, not as accurate as the proponents of drug testing have led the public to believe. Moreover, as stated earlier, only laboratories testing federal employees and laboratories in Rhode Island, Vermont, Louisiana, and Minnesota, need to follow such guidelines and confirm positive results using the gas chromatograph-mass spectrometer. Thus, the majority of testing laboratories need not follow any guidelines concerning confirmation of positive results. When it is used, its true accuracy is not close to what is portrayed by the drug testing industry. Even though it is claimed by some to be almost 100% accurate, human error alone has been shown to cause significant numbers of false positive results (34,65,216,230).

Drug Testing Detects More Than Drugs

People who are not drug users are being denied employment and being labeled as drug users because common foods, over-the-counter preparations and prescription medications are causing them to unknowingly fail drug tests. Employers rarely tell employment candidates that they failed the drug test because it would, no doubt, bring adamant protests by those who were erroneously labeled as drug users and to possible legal challenges by applicants (1,27). Employers would then be required to use much more expensive drug testing methods. Over-the-counter medications that have shown to cause positive drug use results include: most decongestants and cold and allergy medications (47,69-70); diet aids (50,24); cough suppressants(173,38,49,71); sleep aids (29,72); ranitidine (Zantac) (41); anti-nausea medication (72); and vitamin B2 (riboflavin) (72). Most users of these preparations are unaware that they may cause positive results on drug screens.

Prescription medications that cause false positive results include: diet pills such as those used in the Fen-Phen diet; most medications for asthma; NSAIDS; most seizure medication; most medications for anxiety; migraine medication; most medication for insomnia; most pain killers; antidepressants; diuretics; medications to control Parkinson's disease, and some antibiotics (29,38,40,47,64,72). Furthermore, the substances in some of the over-the-counter medications and many prescription medications cannot be differentiated from street drugs even by the gas–chromatograph mass-spectrometer (42,47,64).

A variety of amphetamine analogs that are contained in over-the-counter cold formulations, allergy treatments, and diet aids cause positive drug test results for amphetamines. The Vicks inhaler contains the decongestant 1-methamphetamine, which has approximately one tenth the stimulant potency of d-methamphetamine and causes a positive test that is indistinguishable from methamphetamine use. Because these two compounds give identical mass-spectra, they cannot be differentiated even with the gas chromatograph-mass spectrometer (64,70,73). Also, if urine specimens are left unrefridgerated for extended periods prior to analysis, the formation of phenylethylamine can occur. This product of decomposing, unpreserved urine, can produce a false positive in old unrefridgerated specimens that have not been treated with a fluoride preservative (227).

In 1988, it was shown that nonsteroidal antiinflammatory agents (NSAIDS), such as ibuprofen (Advil, Motrin) and naproxen (Naprosyn) caused immunoassays to test positive for barbiturates, benzodiazepines, and marijuana (74-75). The manufacturers of the tests claimed to have fixed this defect and that it was no longer a problem, but recent studies have shown that NSAIDS at normal doses do cause false positive results (38,42,49,71-72). In 1990, Douglas E. Rollins, M.D., et al, from the Center for Human Toxicology at the University of Utah, showed that urine samples containing ibuprofen and naproxyn produced false positive results for cannabinoids and barbiturates (71). In 1995, Robert E. Joseph, M.D., et al, from the National Institute on Drug Abuse (NIDA), showed that the NSAIDS fenoprofen, flurbiprofen, indometacin, ketoprofen, and tolmetin caused false positive benzodiazepine results (49). Others have also recently reported similar findings with other NSAIDS (42,38). Loyd V. Allen, Ph.D. and Lou M. Stiles, Ph.D., from the University of Oklahoma Health Sciences Center College of Pharmacy, have shown that many common medications can give false positive drug tests: ibuprofen, vitamin B2 (riboflavin), the diuretic ethacrynic acid (Edecrin), the antihistamine promethazine (Phenergan); the antidepressant amitriptyline (Elavil), the gastrointestinal antispasmodic dicyclomine (Bentyl), and the Parkinson's disease treatment trihexyphenidyl (Artane) (72).

People have tested positive for amphetamines, barbiturates, opiates, cocaine, ethanol, and benzodiazepines due to liver problems, kidney problems, and diabetes (39,76-78). A variety of biological metabolites, such as lactate dehydrogenase, lactic acid, maldehydrogen, and protein, can cause a positive drug test if present in above normal concentrations (39). Because the false positive results in these cases are due to a complex interaction of many urinary metabolites and effected by numerous factors including the concentration of substances, the pH, and the salt content, it is not clear how often these substances cause false-positive tests. However, "the fact that some of the diseases that may lead to a false-positive reaction, such as lactic acidosis and diabetes mellitus, are not uncommon suggest that the phenomenon described may not be an extraordinary event (39)." This may be especially problematic for blacks with renal disease because they have a marked elevation of maldehydrogen (a breakdown product of melanin) in their urine (1A).

Poppy seeds are collected from the same plant that produces morphine and codeine and contains both compounds. Following the ingestion of poppy seeds, which are contained in many fast food items and baked goods, significant quantities of morphine and codeine are excreted in the urine for some time (79-86). The ingestion of a single poppy seed bagel or roll can result in levels of codeine and morphine of over 11,500 ng/ml, 38 times the cutoff level, and falsely incriminate someone as an opioid user (70,86). In addition, urines may remain positive for over three days (82-83,86-87).

Codeine (methymorphine) is widely prescribed for many types of pain and discomfort. It is available over-the-counter without a prescription in some states in low concentrations as a cough suppressant. Because the metabolism of codeine, heroin, and poppy seeds all result in morphine, it is usually impossible to determine whether the positive urine resulted from the ingestion of cough medicine, poppy seeds, or heroin (64). Some information can be obtained by measuring the relative amounts of codeine and morphine found in the urine, but no firm conclusions as to the source of the morphine in the urine can be made. If, however, further testing reveals 6-mono-acetelyl-morphine, the by-product unique to heroin, then it is known that the morphine was probably due to heroin use (81). 6-mono-aceteyl-morphine is, however, an unstable molecule and only produced in small quantities; thus, it is usually undetected even among heroin users (88-89). Thus, based on a positive urine opiate test, it is usually impossible to differentiate a heroin user from a person who simply ate a poppy seed bagel. Because testing positive for morphine, regardless of the source, will incriminate a person as a heroin user, federal guidelines require that along with a positive urine test for opioids, clinical signs of opioid abuse must be present before reporting the test as positive (90). The guidelines state that the medical review officer shall determine that there is clinical evidence, in addition to the urine test, of unauthorized use of any opium, opiate, or opium derivative before the test may be ruled positive (91). This requires a face to face interview of the employee by the medical review officer. Again, this guideline only pertains to employees working for a government agency. The overwhelming majority of positive drug tests for opioids are a result of legitimate use of prescription medication or the ingestion of common foods. Unfortunately only those individuals working for a government agency will have the opportunity to explain the reason for the positive test.

Ingestion of substances that have been shown not to cross react and give false positives on drug tests can be metabolized to substances that do cross react, causing false positive drug tests (47). For instance, the manufactures of various over-the-counter medications state, based on testing of the parent compounds, that their preparations do not cross react in the drug tests; but when the drug is ingested and metabolized, substances produced can have high cross reactivity, causing a positive drug test (92). Rafael de la Torre, M.D. states, "It seems that there is a marked difference between results of cross-reactivity studies performed by manufactures on urine specimens spiked with the parent compound and those obtained from healthy subjects given the same compound. The present study confirms that human metabolism contributes to the positive results of some urine samples in cases which the parent compound does not express cross-reactivity with antibodies of the assay (47)." The non-prescription ulcer and heart burn medication ranitidine (Zantac) was thought not to cross react with drug tests, but it has recently been discovered that about half the people taking Zantac will excrete a metabolite that causes drug tests to read positive for amphetamines (41).

Promethazine, which is in many non-prescription sleep aids, anti-nausea medications, and allergy preparations, has been shown to cause a false positive test for marijuana and PCP. The manufactures erroneously claim that it does not cross react in drug tests (72). No doubt, many people have tested positive due to Zantac and Phenergan use, but it has not surfaced because most drug screens are preemployment in nature so the people were not told that they failed the drug screen.

A better measure of cross reactivity of a substance would be to measure the cross reactivity of the natural urinary metabolites, its biological cross reactivity (93). If the biological cross reactivity of common over-the-counter medications were checked, many formulations would show cross reactivity that are currently considered not to have any problems with false positive drug test results (47). "Although many substances might interfere with any assay to produce erroneous results, little is known about what substances do interfere. There has been practically no interest in doing further testing...(10)." Because new medications, which are coming out on a daily basis, are not tested for cross reactivity, numerous people are undoubtedly falsely testing positive.

Numerous studies have shown that passive, second-hand marijuana smoke, be it in a car, at a concert, or at a party, causes positive urine drug tests (95-100). In a study conducted by Edward J. Cone. Ph.D. and the National Institute on Drug Abuse (NIDA), subjects were exposed to 6 hours of passive, second-hand marijuana smoke, as would be likely in a real life situation. The subjects urine subsequently tested positive for, on average, 5 days (129.4 hours) following exposure (99). Because tetrahydrocannabinol (THC), the major psychoactive compound in marijuana, is fat soluble, low level constant exposure to passive, second-hand marijuana smoke is shown to cause the THC to accumulate in the body's fatty tissues to a much greater extent than from the brief periods of intake when marijuana is actively smoked. This accumulation is evidenced by the fact that, in the study by Edward J. Cone, Ph.D. and the National Institute on Drug Abuse, the person with the highest fat content, subject B (86 kg), had a positive urine for the longest time, 9 days following passive, second-hand marijuana exposure (99).

93

Even though the subjects exposed to the passive, second-hand smoke did not feel the effects of the marijuana because the peak THC concentration in the blood was much lower than those who actively smoked, the continuous passive intake of low level fat soluble THC caused the THC to accumulate in the body's fatty tissues. This accumulation resulted in prolonged excretion of THC into the urine, causing positive marijuana drug tests for longer periods of time than if the marijuana was actively smoked (100). On average, subjects who actively smoked one 2.8% THC marijuana cigarette tested positive for 2 days (53 hours), those who actively smoked two 2.8% marijuana cigarettes tested positive for 3 days (69.1 hours), and those exposed to second-hand marijuana smoke tested positive for 5 days (129.4 hours) (100).

Of particular note is the low potency marijuana that was used in the above study. The 2.8% THC used was unrealistically low. In 1993 the average potency for commercial grade marijuana was 4.3%, and the increasing popular Sinsemilla averaged 7.41%. Now, with the widespread popularity of potent hybrid plants, current estimates put the average potency to be upwards of 6% THC, and it is not uncommon to find those in the 14% range (101). Thus, a person would be expected to test positive for marijuana for 7 to 12 days following 6 hours of passive, second-hand exposure, such as would likely be the case at a concert or party. Also, with today's extremely potent strains of marijuana, not only would the detection times be much longer, but it is very likely that even very brief periods of exposure to second-hand marijuana smoke will result in a positive urine test (70). Edward J. Cone, Ph.D., from the National Institute on Drug Abuse states, "Individuals who wish to avoid absorption of a psychoactive substance, such as THC, should avoid environments in which marijuana is combusted (99)." In other words, people should refrain from attending certain concerts or parties because they may be drug tested in the future. It has recently also been shown that passive inhalation of crack cocaine smoke can also give rise to a positive urine cocaine metabolite (102-105)

Cocaine is present on 79% of the U.S. currency (106). It has been shown that handling money can lead to the passive ingestion of enough cocaine to become detectable in the urine. The maximum amount of benzoyleegonine excreted was 72 ng/ml 12.5 hours after handling cocaine contaminated money. This amount is, however, below the 250 ng/ml cutoff and should not cause a positive drug test, if you're lucky.

Legally used medications are most often the cause of positive drug tests, and when employers receive the results of a positive drug test, they are usually not able to distinguish between legitimate medical treatment and drug abuse (107). Laboratories testing federal employees are required to report positive results to a medical review officer (MRO) before notifying the federal employer. The medical review officer is a physician with specific training in drug abuse and drug testing whose function it is to talk with the individual who tested positive. The MRO then determines if the positive result may be due to prescription medication, over-the counter preparations or from another source.

Thus, the medical review officer serves to decrease the number of federal employees falsely accused of drug abuse. In private laboratories doing employment testing, however, the use of an MRO would be financially prohibitive so drug test results from non-federal employees are not reviewed by anyone to determine if the positive drug test could be due to something other than illegal drugs. Consequently, very few prospective employees will ever be allowed the opportunity to explain their positive drug tests (90). Remember, most positive tests are not due to illegal drugs. Consequently, all positive tests are reported to employers who rarely have enough knowledge about drug testing to determine if the positive test was due to illegal drugs, or due to prescription medicine, non-prescription preparations, or from some other source. The employer may fire the employee, eliminate the job candidate, or require the employee or prospective employee to divulge what prescription medication she is taking.

An applicant can state that he is taking over-the-counter or prescription medications on the form submitted with the urine sample which will be given to the employer along with the positive sample. However, because employers are rarely knowledgeable about which medications can give positive results on a drug screen, they usually assume the positive test is due to street drugs. Even if an employer is aware that medications can cross react and cause false positive results, they rarely take the time to differentiate positive tests due to medications from those caused by street drugs. They simply eliminate the candidate from the job pool. More tests are positive due to prescribed medication, over-the-counter preparations, cross reacting food products, and testing apparatus errors than are positive due to illicit drug use. The odds are that your normal manner of living could cause you to test positive and be labeled as a drug abuser without a chance to defend yourself (29,39,72,86,99).

Substances Causing False Positive Drug Tests

This list is not comprehensive; there are other agents not listed that could result in a positive drug test.

Marijuana

Over-the-counter NSAIDS: Ibuprofen; Advil, Nuprin, Mediprim, Motrin, Bayer Select Pain Relief Formula, Excedrin IB Caplets, Genpril, Haltran, Ibuprin, Midol 200, Pamprin, Trendar Cramp Relief Formula, Cramp End Tablets, Medipren, Rufin. Naproxen; Aleve. Ketoprofen; Orudis KT

Prescription NSAIDS: Anaprox, Tolectin, ifenoprofen, flurbiprofen, oxaprozin, Ansaid, Clinoril, Dolobid, Feldene, Indocin, Lodine, Meclomen, Motrin, Nalfon, Naprosyn, Orudis, Relafen, Voltaren.

Over-the-counter allergy preparations, sleep aids, and antinausea medications that contain promethazine: Phenergan, Promethegan.

Riboflavin (vitamin B2), hempseed oil

Kidney infection; kidney disease; diabetes; liver disease

Dronabinol (Marinol), Edecrin

Amphetamines

Over-the-counter cold and allergy remedies that contain ephedrine, pseudoephedrine, propylephedrine, phenylephrine, or desoxyephedrine: Nyquil, Contact, Sudafed, Allerest 12 hour, A.R.M., Triaminic 12, Ornade, Tavist-D, Dimetapp, Sinex, Neosynephrine, Actifed, Bayer Select Maximum Strength Sinus Pain Relief Caplets, Contact Non-Drowsy Formula Sinus Caplets, Dristan Cold Caplets, Maximum Strength Sine-Aid Tablets, Maximum Strength Sudafed Sinus Caplets, Maximum Strength Tylenol Sinus Gelcaps, No Drowsiness Sinarest Tabs, Sinus Excedrin Extra Strength Caplets, Cheracol Sinus, Drixoral Cold and Flu, Efidac/24,

Phenegan-D, Robitussin Cold and Flu, Vicks Nyquil.

Over-the-counter diet aids containing phenylpropanolamine: Dexatrim, Accutrim.

Over-the-counter nasal sprays: Vicks inhaler, Afrin.

Asthma medication: Marax, Bronkaid tablets, Primatine Tablets

Prescription medication: Amfepramone, Cathne, Etafediabe, Morazone, phendimetrazine, phenmetrazine, benzphetamine, fenfluramine, dexfenfluramine, dexdenfluramine, Redux, mephentermine, Mesocarb, methoxyphenamine, phentermine, amineptine, Pholedrine, hydroymethamphetamine, Dexedrine, amifepramone, clobenzorex, fenproyorex, mefenorex, fenelylline, Didrex,

Amphetamines (continued)

dextroamphetamine, methphenidate, Ritalin, pemoline, Cylert, selegiline, Deprenyl, Eldepryl, Famprofazone.

NAISDS (See Marijuana above)

Kidney infection; kidney disease; diabetes; liver disease

Cocaine

Kidney infection; kidney disease; diabetes; liver disease

Amoxicillin, tonic water

Opioids

Poppy seeds; Emprin; Tylenol with codeine; Capital with Codeine; Margesic; the antibiotic rifampicin; Most prescription pain medicine: Vicodin, Percodan, Percocet, Wygesic.

Cough supressants that contain dextromethorphan: Nyquil, Doco Children's Cough syrup, Comtrex, Peda-care, and Benylin.

Kidney infection; kidney disease; diabetes; liver disease

Barbiturates

Fiorinol for tension headaches; some sleeping pills; Donnatol for treatment of irritable bowel syndrome and stomach ulcers; antiasthmatic preperations that contain phenobarbitol; Dilantin

NSAIDS (See marijuana above)

Benzodiazepines

Most prescription sleeping pills and anti-anxiety medicaton.

NSAIDS (See marijuana above)

Kidney infection; kidney disease; diabetes; liver disease

Lyseric acid diethylamide (LSD)

Migraine medication: egotamine, Ergostat, Cafergot, Wigraine, Imitrex,

Hydergine, bromocription, methysergiside, lisuride, lysergol, Artane, triprolidine

The antidepressant amitriptyline (Elavil), the gastrointestional antispasmatic dicyclomine (Bentyl). and the over-the-counter allergy preparations, sleep aids, and antinausea medications that contain promethazine: Phenergan, Promethegan.

Hair Testing: Could It Be More Unjust?

Hair testing is thought by some to be an excellent way to track an individual's drug use because, in theory, when a drug is taken, the drug metabolite is permanently deposited in a discrete segment adjacent to the hair root. This allows laboratories to determine the time of drug use based on the distance the drug was deposited from the follicle and an average hair growth rate of 1.3 cm per month (109). Therefore, if a drug is found in a segment 10.4 cm (4 inches) from the root, it was theoretically taken 8 months ago. However, after ingestion of a drug, the drug metabolite is often distributed over multiple segments extending far from the root, making the single dose appear as frequent multiple doses (109). This is possibly due to the storage of the drug in the hair follicle. Also, hair testing is extremely poor at identifying current drug use because the maximum amount of drug is deposited one to two months after drug use and is often not detectable until weeks after use (109-110).

Racial Bias

Most drugs, including cocaine and marijuana, bind and incorporate into the hair of African-Americans 10 to 50 times greater than drugs are incorporated into the hair of Caucasians (109,111-112). Thus, with equal drug use, African-Americans are 10 to 50 times more likely then Caucasians to have a positive drug test. Robert E. Joseph, M.D., et al, from the National Institute on Drug Abuse (NIDA), writes, "Differences greater than 50 fold were observed in cocaine binding to Africoid male hair compared with blond, female Caucasoid hair specimens (111)." Gary L. Henderson, Ph.D., et al, from the Department of Medical Pharmacology and Toxicology at the University of California, Davis School of Medicine, writes, "A significant variable affecting the incorporation of cocaine into hair appeared to be race...non-caucasians had significantly more cocaine incorporated into their hair than did their Caucasian counterparts (109)." Opioids were shown to incorporate into pigmented hair 21.3 times more than into non pigmented hair following identical doses (112). Greater concentrations of cocaine were also found in the hair of Hispanics and Indians in comparison with Caucasians who received identical doses (109). Other studies have also demonstrated and confirmed the racial bias in hair testing (113-115).

The melanin content varies between ethnic groups, and because melanin can bind drugs, the removal of the melanin prior to analysis is stated by some as a way to remove the racial bias of hair testing (116). It has been found, however, that the removal of the melanin prior to analysis eliminates less than 10% of the bound drugs with 90% of the drugs remaining in the hair. Thus, the removal of the melanin does not affect the ethnic bias of drug testing. Robert E. Joseph, M.D., et al, from the NIDA, writes, "Clearly, removal of the melanin fraction from the hair digest does not eliminate binding differences between different hair types....These findings add to the mounting evidence that suggests that bias can exist in hair testing for drugs of abuse because of selective accumulation of drugs in male Africoid hair (111)."

Contamination

Many studies have shown that hair can easily be rendered positive for illicit drugs by external environmental contamination from substances such as passive, second-hand marijuana smoke (65-66,117-119). D. Blank, Ph.D. and D. Kidwell, Ph.D. write, "Contamination of hair by external sources of drugs, generating false positives, was presented as the major limitation in hair testing.. (117)." Because of the lipophilic (fat soluble) nature of THC, it readily diffuses into the structure of the hair. Thus, when hair is exposed to even minute amounts of external, second-hand marijuana smoke, the THC will be absorbed and become permanently incorporated into the hair resulting in a positive drug test until that portion of the hair is cut off.

The drug cutoff levels with hair testing have been set extremely low so that no drug users would be able to escape detection. In doing so, the lower limits are so low that the minute amounts of drugs that are absorbed by the hair from external second-hand smoke and particulate matter are readily detected. The cocaine vapor from a crack pipe or someone walking down the street with a cigarette sprinkled with heroin can contaminate the hair of those in the area, and the smoke from a few puffs of a marijuana cigarette can permanently contaminate the hair of those inside a large house, auditorium, or concert hall (65). A recent study found that young children living in the homes of crack cocaine users tested postive for cocaine in thier hair. The investigators were unable to differentiate hair rendered positive due to drug use from hair contaminated from cocaine vapor (102).

Drug testing facilities wash the hair before testing in an attempt to decontaminate the hair, but because drug compounds, especially THC, diffuses into the deep layers of the hair, this is usually unsuccessful (66). Edward J. Cone, Ph.D., from the NIDA, was unable to decontaminate hair exposed to opioids or cocaine vapor despite rigorous efforts that were much more extensive than the decontamination procedures used by clinical laboratories. He writes, "After this wash procedure, the hair samples remained highly contaminated. Environmental contamination of hair could occur under a variety of conditions...Smoking heroin could release trace amounts of heroin vapor into the air and contaminate bystanders (65)." Summarizing a similar study, he states, "Samples exposed to cocaine vapor remained heavily contaminated with cocaine after washing (119)."

Repeated shampooing has also shown to have a negligible effect on the drug content of the hair (110). Thus, if a person goes to a concert or a party where marijuana is being smoked, the smoke may permanently contaminate the exposed portions of hair, and if a year later that person is subjected to a hair drug screen, he or she may test positive. Because the hair of African-Americans takes up and incorporates the THC molecules so much more readily than the hair of Caucasians, African-Americans are overwhelmingly more likely than Caucasians to test positive due to external contamination by second-hand marijuana smoke. In fact, African-Americans are over 50 times more likely to falsely be labeled as a marijuana user than a Caucasian, and because the THC incorporates deep into the hair, the external contamination can cause the person to falsely test positive from months to years (110-111,120).

The dyeing of hair also has different effects for different types of hair; hair from African-Americans incorporates more drug into the hair the longer the dyeing treatment while brown and blond hair from Caucasians incorporates less drug with dyeing treatments (117). Bleaching, perming, and UV exposure cause drug levels to decrease (121).

The fact that hair can easily become permeated with a wide variety substances due to external contamination has largely been ignored by the testing industry. An external source such as second-hand marijuana smoke can contaminate hair making it indistinguishable in a laboratory from the hair of an actual marijuana user (66). One director of a drug testing facility, when questioned about cocaine and marijuana contamination of hair for employment testing, stated, "Do you want to hire someone who hangs out in places where these drugs are used?"

After conducting hair drug testing on cadets, the Navy discovered conflicting results between the test and the confidential "self reports" completed by each individual. Without addressing the possibility that the positive tests were due to external contamination, the Navy automatically concluded that the cadets had falsified their confidential "self reports" even though the cadets had nothing to gain by falsifying the reports. They did not consider that the tests actually reflected false positives. They assumed that their tests were 100% accurate before even investigating other possibilities (110).

Pass Them Tests

Clearly, employment drug testing is of no benefit in treating the drug abuse problem in this country. It not only fails to encourage rehabilitation, it actually keeps users from getting the help they need. It does not decrease workplace accidents, and it is not making for a safer workplace. It is often unfair and is being used to illegally discriminate against people who use prescription medication. It is falsely labeling people as drug users, and it is devastating people's lives. Its punitive nature fosters the archaic reactionary belief that drug abuse can be eradicated by force, which only leads this country further away from possible success in the treatment of the drug abuse problem in this

country. I am against its widespread use. Thus, I don't mind discussing the methods people are using to pass drug tests.

Because immunoassays depend upon complex molecular interactions for successful detection of illicit drugs, substances that alter these chemical interactions can render the immunoassay unable to identify drugs in the urine. Illicit drug users have employed a variety of methods to escape detection: including the ingestion of extreme quantities of fluid and adding various adulterating substances to the urine specimen. Some of these methods are discussed.

Water Dilution

Drinking large quantities of water to dilute the urine is a very powerful method used by drug users to lower the urine drug concentration below the cut-off level. The normal kidney has a 6 fold concentrating ability (the kidney is able to produce a urine 6 times more concentrated than normal) and a 4 fold diluting ability (the kidney is able to produce urine that is 4 times more dilute than normal). Thus, drug users can dilute their urine 4 fold by drinking large quantities of water before the test, causing the urine drug concentration to be one fourth the normal value. If this brings the drug concentration below the cut-off level, the urine is read as negative for drugs (1).

The kidneys' concentrating and diluting ability is measured by the urine osmolarity, which normally ranges from 50 to 1200 osmol per liter with 300 osmols per liter being average. A very low specific gravity, signifying a very dilute urine, may arouse suspicion, and a repeat urine may be requested. In reality, the laboratories are much too busy to analyze urine laboratory values, and a dilute urine is rarely questioned, especially if it is a preemployment drug screen. Drinking excessive amounts of water can, however, be dangerous, causing brain edema or exacerbation of congestive heart failure in susceptible people. Some drug users take diuretics, such as furosemide (Lasix), before the test to dilute their urine even further.

Bleach

Liquid bleach when added directly to the urine sample, (bleach should never be ingested; it is extremely dangerous and may cause death), has been shown to oxidize and destroy THC and other cannabinoids, making them undetectable by immunoassay, chromatography, and even mass spectrometry (122-125). Liquid bleach in a 1.2% to 5% final concentration, which would be approximately 1 to 3 cc (1 teaspoon equals 5 cc) of bleach added to the 60 ml urine sample, masked marijuana use by causing false negative marijuana readings for all assay types tested, including EMIT, RIA, and FPIA, and gas chromatography-mass spectrometry (122-124,126). As stated above, the bleach appears to actually destroy the THC, rendering a test negative even by gas chromatograph mass-spectrometry (124,122). In addition, the bleach only slightly decreases the pH of a urine sample at the concentrations tested and thus would not arouse suspicion if the pH is checked (123). Bleach also caused a false negative opiate assay (123).

Visine

Visine has shown to cause a false negative test for marijuana. Visine, at a concentration between 20 and 100 ml per liter, was shown to cause urine THC concentrations of 100 ng per ml (twice the cut-off level) to falsely read negative. This concentration of Visine would correspond to 1.2 ml to 6 ml of Visine in a 60 cc urine sample. Larger concentrations of Visine had less of an effect (127). Because Visine adheres to the walls of a plastic container and this study was done using glass containers, it would require, on average, 1.5 times as much Visine to be added to the urine in a plastic container to expect the same results (118, 129). Therefore, 2 to 3 cc of Visine in a 60 cc sample of urine should be effective.

There is a chemical called benzalkonium in the Visine that surrounds the carboxy-THC molecules in circles called micelles, which hides the carboxy-THC molecules from detection. The benzalkonium molecule has a hydrophobic (repels water) portion and a hydophilic (attracts water) portion. THC also has a "fat loving" hydrophobic region, which is why THC collects in the users fat cells. Because oil and water do not mix, benzalkonium molecules align themselves in circles with their hydrophobic "fat loving" portions pointing towards the center of the circle away from the surrounding water. The fat soluble portion of the carboxy-THC molecule diffuses into this center, causing it to be effectively excluded from the surrounding urine and rendered undetectable (see figure 2).

The micelles optimally form at certain concentrations which is why adding more than 10 cc of Visine to 60 cc of urine reduces its effect. At higher concentrations, the bezalkonium molecules tend to align themselves in sheets that do not effectively exclude the carboxy-THC molecules from the surrounding urine. Because Visine effectively reduces the apparent concentration of only hydophobic "fat-loving" drugs, it has minimal affect on

115

Figure 2

Visine added to urine can cause THC to be undetectable

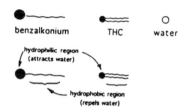

The benzalkonium in the Visine forms micelles in urine

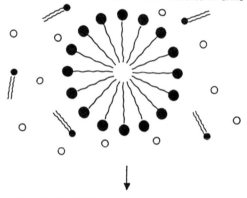

The fat soluable THC molecule diffuses into the oil-like center of the micelle, rendering it undetectable

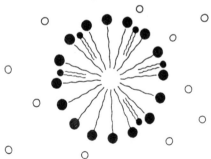

the measured concentrations of benzodiazepines, barbiturates, opioids, cocaine, amphetamines, or phencyclidine The Visine has no effect on pH, density, or appearance of the urine except for slightly reducing its tendency to foam.

Vitamin C

A 1% vitamin C (ascorbic acid) solution, which would be 600 mg of vitamin C in a 60 ml urine sample, has been shown to cause a false negative result for marijuana, amphetamines, and barbiturates (123). Taking 8,000 to 10,000 mg of vitamin C 4 to 6 hours before testing and again 2 hours before the test should be sufficient to mask marijuana use.

The ingestion of large doses of vitamin C also acidifies the urine which will increase the excretion of amphetamines, cocaine, and phencyclidine and will decrease the excretion of phenobarbitol (130). Thus, vitamin C could be used several days before testing to eliminate amphetamines, cocaine, and phencyclidine from the body, but it should not be taken just prior to testing if amphetamines, cocaine, or PCP are present. Taking bicarbonate or antacids such as Tums or Rolaids will decrease the excretion of amphetamines, cocaine, and PCP, which can be useful prior to testing by decreasing

117

the excretion of these substances into the urine. The opposite is true if barbiturates are present; vitamin C taken before a drug test could mask barbiturate use by both altering the assay and by decreasing excretion into the urine.

Aspirin

The ingestion of aspirin (salicylic acid) will reduce the apparent measured concentration of all drugs tested by the EMIT immunoassay. A metabolite of salicylic acid, salicyluric acid, will inhibit the enzyme glucose-6-phospate dehydrogenase, which catalyzes the signal reaction for the EMIT immunoassays, in a dose dependent manner. Thus, the more salicyluric acid in the urine, the less likely a person will test positive because less indicator substance will be formed that signals a positive test. It was shown that a urine salicyluric acid concentration of 300 mg/dl reduced the amount of indicator produced by approximately 60%, and the more salicyluric in the urine, the greater the effect. A urinary concentration of 300 mg/dl of salicyluric acid would be produced by ingesting approximately eight 325 mg aspirin tablets about four hours prior to the test. Adding aspirin directly to the urine does not have any effect because salicylic acid does not inhibit the indicator reaction; it must first be metablized in the body to salicyluric acid (41).

Golden Seal

Golden seal root, which contains hydrastine and berberine, can decrease the urine THC concentration if the golden seal is present in high concentrations (125). The required golden seal concentration is much too high to be obtained by taking golden seal by mouth, as in drinking a tea or by taking capsules containing the herb. If added directly to the urine in a concentration of over 30 mg per ml, it can lower the THC level enough to cause a false negative, but when directly added to the urine at this high concentration, it turns the urine brown. The main component of many herbal detox and drug masking teas is golden seal; as stated above, there is no effective method to obtain a high enough golden seal concentration in the urine to alter the test.

Detox tea

Fifty herbal masking teas were tested, some of which were "guaranteed" to work, but none were able to alter the test (133). The only reason people believe they work is that they all recommend drinking plenty of water with their product which often dilutes the urine enough to cause a negative reading for a borderline drug concentration. Water dilution, as mentioned earlier, is indeed a powerful tool that can be used to pass a drug test. I have received calls from people who failed a drug test after using the "guaranteed" commercial detox products. After sending their test results to the manufacturers for their "double or triple money back guarantee", they either received letters stating something about drugs being illegal, or they received no reply at all.

Klear

Klear is a commercial product that claims to mask THC when added directly to the urine. Based on anecdotal reports and from results of small semi-experimental studies, it appears to have mixed results. Some claim that it only works on the EMIT immunoassay while others claim its active ingredient is potassium nitrate, which interferes with the confirmatory GC-MS analysis. Either way, its ability to mask marijuana use is at best mixed.

Drano

Liquid Drano when added directly to a urine sample (Drano should never be ingested; it is extremely dangerous and may cause death), has been shown to cause false negative drug tests for cocaine, barbiturates, amphetamines, opiates, and marijuana. This effect is achieved at concentrations between 12 ml per liter and 42 ml per liter which would be approximately 1 to 2 cc in a

60 cc sample. The Drano, however, bubbles and fizzes when first added to urine, which would be difficult to explain. It also causes the urine pH, which is sometimes checked, to increase outside the normal physiologic range (124).

Salt

Salt (NaCl) when added to a urine sample to achieve a concentration of 50 to 75 mg per ml, which would be 3 to 9 grams in a 60 ml urine specimen, has been shown to cause false negative tests for amphetamines, barbiturates, cocaine, opiates, and marijuana (123,126).

Liquid Soap

Liquid soap at a concentration of 12 to 23 ml per liter, which would be approximately 1 to 2 cc of liquid soap in a 60 ml urine sample, caused false negative results for marijuana, barbiturates, benzodiazepines, and PCP (124-126).

Vinegar

Vinegar at a minimum concentration of 125 ml per liter, which would be 7.5 cc of vinegar in 60 ml of urine, has been shown to cause a false negative test for marijuana

121

(124-126). When vinegar is ingested, however, its acidic nature is quickly buffered making it unlikely to affect drug testing assays.

Tolmetin

Tolmetin, a prescription NSAID like ibuprofen, has been shown to cause a false negative test for cannabinoids and opioids (49). Tolmetin would probably also mask use of cocaine, amphetamines, and barbiturates, as well.

Ciprofloxicin

The common antibiotic ciprofloxicin has been shown to potentially cause opiates, cocaine, amphetamines, and benzodiazepines to be undetected by immunoassay (131).

Metronidazole

Metronidazole, an antibiotic used to treat vaginal infections, has shown to mask assay detection of all illicit drugs tested at a concentration of 500 ug per ml, which would be 30 mg in a 60 ml urine sample (132). 30 mg of metronidazole is contained in 4 grams of metronidazole vaginal suppository (one applicator full).

Direct water dilution

Diluting the urine with toilet water rarely works. Many drug testing facilities color the toilet water for this reason. Also, if the temperature of the urine is checked, it will be lower than body temperature due to the addition of room temperature toilet water (91), and the specific gravity will fall below the normal physiologic range (1). Use of saline solution for sample dilution has been used with some success. A 125-250 cc bag can be purchased in medical supply houses. Addition of saline will not cause the specific gravity to be abnormal.

Substitute urine

Substituting clean urine for the donor's own urine has worked depending upon the circumstances and how closely the person is monitored while urinating. A person taking a preemployment drug test will most likely be allowed more privacy than a person taking a drug test while in rehabilitation. Obviously, the substituted urine must be drug free, and it must also be kept close enough to the body so it will be within 2-3 degrees of body temperature to avoid detection when the temperature is measured. A temperature strip is sometimes embedded in the plastic cup. It should be between 94 and 99 degrees centigrade.

People have gone as far as placing clean urine in a balloon with a tube taped to the underside of their penis or actually infusing another person's urine into their bladder via a catheter prior to the test. Abbie Hoffman, activist for drug law reform, describes in his 1987 book, Steal this Urine Test, a technique of using a reservoir-tipped, non-lubricated condom. He suggests filling one and placing a second one over it, to prevent breakage, and taping it close to the crotch. Women can place it in their Vaginas. When it is time to give the sample, he advises his readers to use a presharpened fingernail to puncture the tip (237). Also, for people that do not want to ask for another person's urine or don't know of anyone suitable, there is commercially available freeze dried urine, to which you just add warm water.

Cutoff Urine Drug Concentrations (ng/ml)

Drug	Immunoassay	GC-MS
Marijuana metabolite (a)	50	15
Cocaine metabolite (b)	300	250
Opioid metabolite	300 (c)	150 (d)
Phencyclidine	25	25
Amphetamine	1000 (e)	500 (f)
Methamphetamine	1000 (e)	500 (f)
Benzodiazepines	300	200

-

(a) Delta 9-tetrahydrocannabinol-9-carboxylic acid.
(b) Benzoylecgonine
(c) Total conjugated opiates
(d) Morphine or codeine
(e)Total amphetamines
(f) d-amphetamine or methamphetamine

Approximate Time Intervals for Detection of Drugs in the Urine After Use

Drug Tested	Days Detectable After Use
Marijuana metabolite (a)	
Single use	1-11
Chronic us	7-30
Cocaine metabolite (b)	1-3
Opioid metabolite (c)	1-2
Phencyclidine	3-7
Amphetamines	1-3
Methamphetamine	1-4
Barbiturates	
Short and intermediate acting	1-7
Long acting (phenobarbitol)	10-30
Benzodiazepines	1-5

-

(a) Delta 9-tetrahydrocannabinol-9-carboxylic acid.
(b) Benzoylecgonine

Legal Concerns

Major legal concerns include the right to be protected against unreasonable search and seizure, the right to procedural due process, and the right to equal protection under the law (163).

Unreasonable Search and Seizure

The Fourth Amendment to the U.S. Constitution guarantees the "right of the people to be secure in their personal houses, paper and effects against unreasonable search and seizure" except upon probable cause (166). Many courts have ruled that to require a urine sample to be analyzed is a search under the Fourth Amendment

(167). Thus, the probable cause requirement has been at issue for random drug testing of federal employees.

Indiscriminate drug testing threatens traditional Fourth Amendment values, which perhaps more than any other provision of the Bill of Rights expresses an essential quality of democracy, the defense of personal dignity against violation by the state. We ought not to experiment with these rights. They are fragile. Once damaged they are not easily repaired. Once lost they are not easily recovered. "Adherence to tested Fourth Amendment principles is particularly important when, as now, there is widespread clamor for a simple solution to a serious social problem. The saddest episodes in American constitutional history have been those occasions, such as the internment of Americans of Japanese descent during World War II, when we have bent our principles to the zealotry of the moment. What is expedient is not necessarily fair, or constitutional (234)."

The American Civil Liberties Union (ACLU) opposes indiscriminate drug testing because they believe it is unfair and unreasonable to force millions of workers who are not even suspected of using drugs and whose job performance is satisfactory, to submit to degrading and intrusive urine tests on a regular basis. The ACLU questions the fairness of treating the innocent and the guilty alike (235). U.S. Supreme Court Justice Antonin Scalia states, "The impairment of individual liberties cannot be the means of making a point...Symbolism, even symbolism for so worthy a cause as the abolition of unlawful drugs, cannot validate an otherwise unreasonable search (215)." "Random or mass urine testing reverses the presumption of innocence upon which much of our jurisprudence is built, and it violates the strong prohibition of dragnet searches sweeping in the many who are innocent in order to find the few who are guilty which is the hallmark of a free and democratic society...If the lessons of history are to teach us anything, it is that we must be vigilant against public hysteria of the moment and adhere to basic constitutional principles and democratic values which are the hallmarks of a free society. The drug problem though real, must be distinguished from the drug testing problem (236)."

Some argue that if you don't use drugs, you have nothing to hide--so why object to testing? But innocent people do have something to hide: their private life. The right to be left alone is, in the words of the late Supreme Court Justice Louis Brande is, "the most comprehensive of rights and the right most valued by civilized men." The right to privacy is, as determined by the U.S. Supreme

Court, to be an implicit guarantee of the Constitution (164). Consent is normally required before someone can invade your privacy by probing into your medical records, yet drug tests reveal numerous physiological facts about a person that should not necessarily be shared with others. Drug tests can reveal the use of contraceptives, pregnancy, or medication for depression, epilepsy, diabetes, insomnia, schizophrenia, high blood pressure, and heart trouble.

Disclosure of the information from drug testing can be embarrassing and can lead to loss of employment, financial ruin, discrimination, and to further disclosure of medical information. Drug testing forces individuals to lose all control over who has access to their confidential medical information. It is not unreasonable to maintain that employees should be free from scrutiny during their non-working hours as long as their activities are not affecting their work performance. Federal Judge H. Lee Sarokin acknowledged that there is a drug problem in America, but saw drug testing as a graver threat: "In order to win the war against drugs, we must not sacrifice the life of the constitution in the battle...We would be appalled at the spectre of the police spying on employees during their free time and then reporting their activities to their employers. Drug testing is a form of surveillance, albeit a technological one. Nonetheless, it reports on a person's off-duty activities just as surely as if someone had been present and watching. It is George Orwell's Big Brother Society come to life (222)." A federal district judge in New Orleans ruled against a U.S. Customs Service program that required employees seeking promotions to certain positions to undergo urinalysis. He stated the practice as "utterly repugnant to the Constitution." Judge Robert F. Collins said that, in addition to violating the Fourth Amendment, the program invaded the general "zone of privacy created by several fundamental constitutional guarantees (214)."

Appellate courts have, in general, upheld screening urinalysis if testing involves government employees in positions dealing with public safety (168). But in April 1997, the Supreme Court ruled 8-1 in *Chandler et al v. Miller, Governor of Georgia et al,* that drug testing of political candidates is unconstitutional. The Court recognized that indiscriminate drug screening of political candidates makes no scientific sense and ruled that government-initiated suspicionless drug testing of political candidates for symbolic purposes, however well-intended, violates the Constitution (191).

Due Process

The Fourth Amendment to the Constitution guarantees that "no person...be deprived of life, liberty, or property without due process of the law...(166)." However, an employer need not give an employee or prospective employee the opportunity to rebut the results of the test. The job seeker is immediately eliminated from the applicant pool often without knowing it was due to a positive drug test. Many of these positive tests are due to substances other than illicit drugs, but instead of spending additional time and money to delineate true positive drug tests from the false positive drug tests, it is much easier for the employer to simply eliminate all positive testing job candidates from the applicant pool. If employers were to tell every applicant whose urine came up positive the true reason for being eliminated, it would cost them time and money having to defend their testing procedures and results. For these reasons, most people who are eliminated by preemployment drug testing are not told that they tested positive. They are either given a bogus reason or no reason at all. The candidate is not allowed the opportunity to explain a positive test that was due to a prescription medication or certain foods (i.e. a poppy seed bagel). Many people who are finding it difficult to obtain a job may be unaware that they are testing positive due to prescription or over-the-counter medications.

Employers have also found drug testing to be an easy way to look into a candidate's medical history. Based on illegally obtained confidential medical information, employers are eliminating job candidates and forcing employees out of jobs. A company may not hire a person or eliminate an employee if they take medication for depression, anxiety, insomnia, high blood pressure, high cholesterol. Anything an employer finds by conducting drug tests that he or she feels may adversely affect job performance, increase sick leave, or possibly cause a person to use health benefits and raise the company's insurance premiums, may be used to justify an employee's termination. In short, drug testing allows employers to discriminate based on confidential health information (19).

Equal Protection Under the Law

Testing a group of persons without prior suspicion may lead to an allegation of bias or an absence of equal protection under the law. The Fourteenth Amendment was cited as protection against selection of a group of athletes for testing by the National Collegiate Athletic Association

(NCAA) without demonstrating a likelihood that drug use was prevalent in that population (169).

Equal protection under the law is addressed by the 14th Amendment to the U.S. Constitution, and discrimination is addressed in the Civil Rights Act of 1964 and the Rehabilitation Act of 1973 (163). The Rehabilitation Act makes it illegal for an employer to terminate an employee in rehabilitation due to drug use and states that an employer may only test a government employee in rehabilitation for medical reasons (170). Once a government employee is in rehabilitation, he or she cannot be terminated and must be given the opportunity to go back to work and have his performance reevaluated (171-172).

Drugs

Marijuana

The term "cannabinoids" refers to a group of more than 60 compounds found in the plant Cannabis Sativa and includes the marijuana metabolites produced in humans. The most extensively studied cannabinoid is delta-9-tetrahydrocannabinol (THC) (134). THC is also the major and most active psychoactive compound in marijuana (135). In the 1970's, the average THC content of marijuana in the United States was 1%, and as stated earlier, in 1993 the average potency for commercial grade marijuana was 4.3% and the increasing popular Sinsemilla averaged 7.41%. Now, with the widespread popularity of potent hybrid plants, current estimates put the average potency to be upwards of 6% THC, and it is not uncommon to find those in the 14% range (101).

When marijuana is smoked, its effects appear within minutes and usually last for 2 to 3 hours. Oral intake (i.e., eating hash brownies) delays the onset of effect for 30 minutes to 2 hours, but the effects last longer (24). The effects are highly variable and are affected by dose, THC content, experience of the user, and smoking technique. There is usually an altered perception of time, a sense of euphoria, a keener sense of hearing, and more vivid visual imagery. Frequently, there is associated hunger, dry mouth, short term memory impairment, increased pulse, and conjunctival (whites of eyes) reddening. Higher doses can cause paranoia, hallucinations, and delusions. The predominant effects of marijuana on behavior and physiology generally last less than 4 hours after smoking a marijuana cigarette. Chronic use can cause an increase in a variety of cancers, memory impairment, depression, and an Amotivational Syndrome: consisting of apathy, impaired judgment, and loss of ambition (140).

THC is a fat soluble molecule that accumulates in the fatty tissues of the body including the liver and lung and is only slowly released from this depot over time, especially with chronic use (141-142). THC is metabolized to 11-nor-delta-9-tetrahydrocannabinol-9-carboxylic acid (Carboxy-THC). Because THC continually enters the bloodstream from tissue stores, carboxy-THC is excreted in the urine long after the person has stopped using marijuana. Urine of marijuana users can produce positive results from days to weeks after last use depending upon the dose, route, frequency of use, and the timing of the urine collection. Exceptionally long detection times have been recorded in chronic, heavy marijuana users after abstinence (142,144). In one study, George Ellis, Ph.D. et al, found that chronic heavy marijuana users required 2 to 4 weeks of abstinence after smoking one marijuana cigarette to test negative while occasional users required 5 to 11 days of abstinence after one marijuana cigarette. It took 77 days for one exceptionally heavy marijuana user to produce 10 consecutive negative specimens (cutoff 20 ug per ml) after stopping his marijuana use. An individual may produce specimens that test positive, then negative, then positive again over time without additional use (144).

In a study by Marilyn A. Huestis, Ph.D. et al, from the Addiction Research Center of the National Institute on Drug Abuse (NIDA), the average detection time after smoking a low dose (1.75% THC) marijuana cigarette was 3/4 of a day (18.7 hours) and after smoking a high dose

(3.55% THC) marijuana cigarette, the detection time was just under 2 days (45.7 hours). The average detection times varied considerably between subjects despite attempts to standardize marijuana dosing. After smoking the low dose (1.75% THC) marijuana cigarette, detection times varied among subjects from 4.3 hours to 39.1 hours. After smoking the high dose (3.55% THC) marijuana cigarette, detection times varied among subjects from 1 to 2 1/2 days (26.8 to 62.5 hours) (44). Detection times also varied considerably between differing brands of commercial assays on identical specimens. Detection times measured on the same individual using different commercial brands of assays varied by as much as 1.7 days (40.3 hours) (44). Edward J. Cone, Ph.D., from the NIDA, found detection times after one or two 2.8% THC marijuana cigarettes to be 2 days (53 hours) and just under 3 days (69 hours); respectively (145). P. Kelly, Ph.D. and R. Jones, Ph.D. reported detection times by GC-MS (15 ng per ml) of up to 3 days with infrequent users and up to 4 days with frequent users following the injection of a 5 mg THC dose (56). After oral ingestion of marijuana, the THC detection time is usually prolonged: lasting 5 to 12 days depending on the dose (100,146-147). It should be noted that these studies were done with relatively low potency marijuana (THC content between 1.75 and

3.55%). The more potent strains of marijuana used today would prolong the above detection times.

Cocaine

Cocaine (benzoylmethlyegonine C17H21NO4) is prepared from the leaves of the Erythroxylon Coca or Coca plant, which is indigenous to Peru and Bolivia. Cocaine hydrochloride, which is sold as a powder, is prepared by dissolving the cocaine alkaloid from the Coca plant in hydrochloric acid to form a water soluble salt. Cocaine hydrochloride is often converted back to the alkaloid (freebase or crack) by dissolving the cocaine hydrochloride in water with baking soda. A solvent such as ether is sometimes used to extract the cocaine, or the water is evaporated off leaving highly pure cocaine crystals referred to as crack (148).

Cocaine is usually administered intranasally (snorting), intravenously (IV), or by smoking freebase cocaine (crack). When snorted, the bioavailability (the percentage absorbed into the body) is 30-40% (149). Cocaine is quickly absorbed via the nasal route. The absorption is somewhat delayed via the oral route, and almost instantaneous when smoked or administered intravenously. Cocaine reaches the brain within three minutes when snorted, twenty seconds when taken intravenously, and within ten seconds when smoked. It is broken down into two major metabolites: ecgonine methyl ester (EME) and benzoylecgonine, which are detectable in the urine for fourteen to sixty hours after use (24).

Cocaine has two main functions: its main function is stimulation of the central nervous system; its second function is as a local anesthetic by blocking nerve conduction. Its stimulation of the central nervous system is first manifested as a feeling of well-being, euphoria, arousal, self-confidence, relief of boredom and fatigue, and sometimes dysphoria (severe anxiety). The heart speeds up and squeezes harder, and the blood vessels constrict causing an increase in blood pressure. It also commonly causes the pupils to dilate, the muscles to twitch, and the body temperature to rise (150). With chronic use or higher doses of cocaine, the euphoric feelings are often replaced with anxiety, agitation, irritability, psychotic thoughts, and profound paranoia. A chronic user will often begin to experience auditory, visual and tactile hallucinations. Common hallucinations include: imaginary people who are out to get the user; seeing and hearing imaginary police; and seeing bugs on or under the skin, which chronic users may attempt to dig out of their skin or present to an emergency room requesting treatment. It often takes chronic cocaine or methamphetamine use to induce hallucinations, but once they occur, they will likely recur with even small subsequent doses. Due to its local anesthetic properties, the most common cocaine associated medical problem is dental cavities and abscesses. Users do not feel the pain that would normally alert them of a dental problem. Chronic cocaine users are commonly malnourished and suffer from multiple vitamin deficiencies. Chronic intranasal cocaine causes prolonged intense vasoconstriction of the nasal mucosa which can lead to nasal tissue and septum destruction from lack of blood flow. When the cocaine wears off, the vessels dilate which produces sniffles and runny nose (152). The brains of chronic cocaine users become unable to produce sufficient quantities of the neurotransmitters that induce normal feelings of happiness. Thus, as soon as chronic cocaine use is stopped, the person becomes depressed. Cocaine use then becomes their only relief from the depression, and thus begins the vicious cycle: the person's only relief from depression is cocaine, which then makes them more depressed. The user is thrust into a deeper and deeper depression with feelings of helplessness and hopelessness.

Intravenous cocaine users often develop skin infections and abscesses, but even worse, severe infections can occur in their heart, lungs, and brain. Intravenous users who share needles also expose themselves to hepatitis and HIV infection (151). Cocaine can also cause sudden death. The lethal dose is reported to be 1.2 grams, although sudden death can occur after as little as 0.02 grams, which is the dose of the average snort. Cocaine related emergency room visits have skyrocketed in recent years. Death usually occurs because of cardiac arrhythmias (heart attack), continuous epileptic seizures, stroke, and respiratory failure. People may have unknown preexisting conditions and unknowingly be candidates for cocaine related emergencies (151). Amongst women who use cocaine during pregnancy, there is a higher risk of spontaneous abortion, congenital malformations, neurobehavioral impairment, and perinatal morbidity and mortality (149).

Amphetamines

Methamphetamine use is on the rise; methamphetamine related deaths in San Francisco rose 22% between 1993 and 1994. In Los Angeles, 19% of drug abuse deaths in 1995 were due to methamphetamine, compared to only 1% two years prior (153). Moderate doses of amphetamines usually elevate mood, decrease appetite, and produce feelings of increased energy and alertness. They also cause people to become anxious, nervous, and irritable and frequently cause insomnia, restlessness, agitation, and mental instability (152). Chronic use often results in a psychosis that resembles schizophrenia. The user becomes very paranoid with vivid visual and auditory hallucinations. This is often more profound than the cocaine psychosis discussed earlier. Common hallucinations include: imaginary people who are out to get the user; seeing and hearing imaginary police; and seeing bugs on or under the skin. After a person becomes paranoid from chronic amphetamine use, the paranoia will often recur even with subsequent small doses. Chronic users often become obsessed with cleaning, organizing, building, and repairing things, usually working throughout all hours of the night into the early morning (24). Users exhibiting such behaviors are sometimes referred to as "tweakers". Other side effects include: cardiac arrhythmias, high blood pressure, stroke, vomiting, abdominal pain, and dehydration. Convulsions, coma, and death may also result from excessive amphetamine and methamphetamine use. Discontinuation of chronic use of amphetamines, like cocaine, usually causes fatigue, lethargy, and depression (152).

Amphetamines are still prescribed for weight loss, hyperactive children, and narcolepsy (154). Current street names for amphetamines and methamphetamine include uppers, pep pills, bennies, meth, crank, dexies, hearts, ice, black beauties, speed, and crystal. After oral ingestion, peak amphetamine concentration is reached in approximately two hours. Taking antacids to alkalinize the urine decreases excretion into the urine. Taking vitamin C to acidify the urine increases the drug's excretion into the urine (24).

Barbiturates

Barbiturates are potent central nervous system depressants. Commonly used barbiturates include: amobarbitol (Amytal), secobarbitol (Seconnal), pentobarbitol (Nembutal), phenobarbitol (luminal), and butalbital (Fiorinal). Common street names include barbs, downers, goofballs, blues, yellow jackets, red devils, and rainbows (24). Barbiturates have various clinical uses based on their duration of action: the ultrashort-acting thiopental is for induction of anesthesia; the short to intermediate-acting amobarbital and secbarbital are for sedation and sleep; and the long acting agents like phenobarbital are for controlling epileptic seizures (24). At low doses, barbiturates generally induce a state of relaxation, euphoria, and tranquillity. They can impair cognitive and motor function and may cause nausea and abdominal pain. Moderate doses of barbiturates induce anesthesia and can depress respiratory centers in the brain to such an extent to cause death.

Tolerance to barbiturates develops rapidly. It is not uncommon for a user to require 4-5 times the usual dose. Even though the chronic user requires larger and larger doses to achieve the same effect, the lethal dose does not change, which narrows the margin between the desired effect and death. Fortunately, tolerance to the anticonvulsant properties does not appear to occur (155). There is a high degree of cross tolerance between barbiturates and other sedative-hypnotic drugs such as benzodiazepines and alcohol. A person who takes barbiturates will require higher doses of benzodiazepines like Valium and higher doses of alcohol to achieve the same effect. After using barbiturates, it is common for a person to feel "hangover" effects. Abrupt withdrawal from barbiturates can be severe enough to cause death. The barbiturate withdrawal syndrome includes tremulousness (tremors), anxiety, weakness, insomnia, and convulsions (155).

The detection time for barbiturates varies widely depending upon the barbiturate type, its dosage, its rate of accumulation, metabolism, and elimination. It can be detected in the urine after a dose for as short as a day or as long as a month. As would be expected, the short acting barbiturates are usually detectable for a relatively short time and the longer acting barbiturates are detectable for a relatively longer time (156-158). Phenobarbital has been shown to be detectable in the urine for up to 38 days (157). Osmotic diuresis (the taking of diuretics) and the alkalization of urine (taking antacids) significantly increases the excretion of barbiturates into the urine. Immunoassays are sensitive to barbiturates in general but do not identify the specific types. Currently, most immunoassays are based on an antibody to secobarbitol which cross reacts to other barbiturates to varying degrees. For instance, the detection of phenobarbital is 4 times less sensitive than it is for secobarbitol, which can cause false negatives for phenobarbitol (24).

Benzodiazepines

Benzodiazepines are used as sedative-hypnotics, anxiolytics (anti-anxiety drugs), and anticonvulsants (antiseizure medication). Popular benzodiazepines include: Valium (diazepam), Xanax (alprazolam), Halcion (triazolam), Serax (oxazepam), Ativan (lorazepam), Librium (chlordiazepoxide), and Restoril (temazepam). All sedative-hypnotic drugs, which include benzodiazepines, barbiturates, and alcohol, are cross tolerant, meaning that a tolerance developed to one drug will be developed to the other sedative-hypnotic drugs (12). Benzodiazepines produce drunken like behavior which may include: impaired motor control, unsteady walk, mood swings, aggressiveness, impulsivity, slurred speech, ocular myoclonus (jerky eye movements), and impaired judgment. The user feels less anxious and more self-confident. Sedative-hypnotics can cause a fatal overdose and are particularly dangerous when combined with alcohol. Signs of an overdose include shallow respirations, clammy skin, weak pulse, coma, and death. Abrupt withdrawal may cause anxiety, insomnia, tremors, convulsions, delirium, and death. After oral ingestion, peak blood concentrations are reached in 30 to 240 minutes. Many factors can influence the metabolism of benzodiazepines and thus influence their duration of action and detection. Factors that increase the duration of action and detection include: increased age, disease states (especially liver disease), and the use of other drugs, especially those medications that inhibit oxidative metabolism of the benzodiazepines like cimetidine (Zantac) (24).

Psychedelics

The term "psychedelic" was coined in the 1950's to mean a consciousness expanding (12). They generally include drugs that cause an altered state of consciousness resembling psychosis. The term "hallucinogenic" is used for substances that produce visual, auditory, tactile, gustatory, and olfactory hallucinations (hallucinations of

149

the senses). The psychedelic drug phencyclidine (PCP) was originally used for surgical anesthesia because it caused no significant cardiovascular or respiratory depression, but it was abandoned because patients experienced postoperative agitation, hallucinations, and mental disturbances (24). Because of its easy synthesis from readily available starting chemicals, amateur laboratories prepare quantities of PCP that often vary in purity for the illicit drug trade. Psychedelics or hallucinogens include LSD (acid), phencyclidine (PCP, Angle Dust), MDA, MDMA (Ecstasy), and dextramethorphan (over-the-counter cough suppressant). Marijuana is sometimes placed in this category. The duration of these drugs' effects can be from a few minutes to several days.

Phencyclidine (PCP) has variable and unpredictable effects. Depending upon the amount used, PCP can cause euphoria, relaxation, pleasant stimulation, sensations of weightlessness and immense strength, distortion of time and space, feelings of disassociation from environment, visual and auditory distortions, difficulties in thinking, anxiety, panic, bizarre illusions, paranoia, and amnesia. The paranoia coupled with an altered sense of reality can provoke bizarre and violent behavior (161). Chronic use of psychedelics can cause prolonged psychotic reactions with flashbacks, exacerbations of preexisting psychiatric illness, prolonged and possibly severe depression, speech difficulties, thought processing disorders, impaired memory, loss of ambition, emotional flatness, detachment, and anxiety. These symptoms tend to fade as drug free time increases (12). Users may go for days without food or sleep with a subsequent "crash" where they feel depressed, disoriented, and lethargic. Flashbacks have been reported after PCP use is discontinued. Death has been reported in association with PCP use, but this may have been due to resultant behavior following use rather than the toxic effects of PCP. Some tolerance develops with chronic use, but physical addiction is uncertain. Withdrawal symptoms have not been reported with psychedelics (24). Phencyclidine may be taken orally or smoked. When PCP is smoked, it is usually mixed with marijuana with the effects usually lasting 4 to 6 hours (162). Phencyclidine is metabolized to 4-phenyl-4 hydroxpiperdine and then excreted into the urine after conjugation to form a glucuronide, which can be detected for 1 to 7 days after use. Acidification of the urine with vitamin C hastens excretion from the body (24).

Addiction Defined

Physical dependence is a process of pharmacological adaptation at the cellular level to the presence of a substance with a predictable "withdrawal" response when the substance is abruptly discontinued. Physical dependence is sometimes present with addiction, but often times it is not. People can also experience physical dependence and not be addicted; those who use pain killers for chronic pain or barbiturates for the control for epilepsy experience withdrawal symptoms if their medication is abruptly discontinued, but they are not addicted (19). Addictive disease is a pathological state with characteristic signs and symptoms as well as a predictable outcome if left untreated. It is characterized by a compulsive desire for the drug; loss of control when using the drug; denial of both use and the negative consequences of use; continued use in spite of the adverse consequences; denial; and the possibility of relapse after stopping drug use (12). It is the persistent use of a psychoactive drug that is seriously interfering with an individual's economic, health, or social functioning (20). Addiction is a complex disease that effects the addict and the addict's friends and family (21). People wrongly equate addiction with physical dependence. Again, dependence may or may not be present with addiction. Drug abusers wrongly assume that if they are not physically dependent upon drugs, they are not addicted. Likewise, people believe detoxification and abstinence are the treatments for addiction, but they are only the first steps to recovery from drug or alcohol addiction.

The term recovery, as used in 12 step programs such as Alcoholics Anonymous, refers to a person's state of being: acceptance of alcoholism or drug addiction as a disease and maintenance of sobriety through active avoidance of drugs and alcohol by using peer support and adherence to the 12-step program. Recovery is a continual, dynamic, ongoing process that is pragmatically useful and a valuable concept in the treatment of alcoholism and drug addiction (12). Addiction is a progressive, incurable disease that can, however, be brought into remission through abstinence from drugs and alcohol and lifelong commitment to the recovery process. Recovery from alcohol and drug abuse is much more than not using. Drugs and alcohol are not the addicts' problems; they are the solutions used by the addicts and the alcoholics to their problems. While abstinent from drugs and alcohol, addicts must work on their problems of hate, insecurity, guilt, shame, and poor self-esteem. Twelve step recovery programs are designed to do just that. By utilizing a twelve step program, addicts and alcoholics can find the happiness, serenity, love, self-worth, and inner peace that they had once sought through drugs and alcohol but found fleeting at best.

Unfortunately, those who fail their preemployment drug test will probably not have the financial resources to pay for and enter a recovery and rehabilitation program. This is a tragedy and hurts me deeply; these people are denied treatment which is their only chance to truly be happy. They are forced to continue suffering by being denied treatment for their disease. Employment can give the addict the financial means or medical insurance to enter a rehabilitation and recovery program that would otherwise be impossible. Hopefully, along with educating the general public about the destructive affect drug testing has on the members of society, including those who don't use drugs, this book will enable or prompt the addict or alcoholic to get help in a twelve step recovery program and escape the living hell of addiction.

References

1. Osterloh JD, Becker CE. Chemical dependency and drug testing in the workplace. J Psychoactive Drugs 1990;22:407-17.

2. Allgulander CA, Evanoff B. Psychiatric diagnoses and perceived health problems in a sample of working swedes treated with psychoactive medications. J of Psychoactive Drugs 1990;22:467-78.

3. Greenblatt DJ, Shade East Thomas Road   Suite #1077J Clin Psychopharmacol 1990;10:157–9.

4. McBay AJ, Hudson P. Cost-effective drug testing. J Forensic Sci 1987;32:575-9.

5. Greenblatt DJ. Urine drug testing: what does it test? N Engl Law Rev 1989;23:651-66.

6. Glantz LH. A nation of suspects: drug testing and the Fourth Amendment. Am J Public Health 1989;79:1427-31.

7. Curran WJ. Compulsory drug testing: the legal barriers. N Engl J Med 1987;316:318-21.

8. AMA Council on Scientific Affairs. Issues in employee drug testing. JAMA 1987;258:2089-96.

9. Walsh CD, Elinson L, Gostin L. Worksite drug testing. Annu Rev Publ Health 1992;13:197-221.

10. McBay AJ. Drug-analysis technology-pitfalls and problems of drug testing. Clin Chem 1987;33:33B-40B.

11. American Medical Association Council on Scientific Affairs. Scientific issues in drug testing. JAMA 1987;257:3110-4.

12. Seymour RB, Smith DE. Identifying and responding to drug abuse in the workplace: An overview. J Psychactive Drugs 1990;22:383-405.

13. Smith DE, Editor's introduction. Therapeutic Drugs and drugs of abuse in the era of the drug-free workplace. J Psychoactive Drugs 1990;22:381-2.

14. Anglin MD, Westland CA. Drug monitoring in the workplace: Results from the California commercial laboratory drug testing project 1989. In: Gust SW, Walsh JM, eds. Drugs in the Workplace: Reseach and Evaluation Data. NIDA Reasearch Monograph 1991. Rockville, Maryland: NIDA.

15. Federal Drug Free Workplace Survey. Subcommittee on Treasury, Postal Service, and General Government, Committee on Appropriations, U.S. Senate, Jan 18, 1991. U.S. General Accounting Office, GGD-91-25.

16. Lundberg GD. Mandatory unindicated urine drug screening. Still Chemical McCarthyism. JAMA 1986;256:3003-5.

17. Morgan JP. Problems of mass urine screening for misused drugs. J of Psychoactive Drugs 1984;16:305-17.

18. Levy D. USA Today. Dec 20, 1996.

19. DuPont RL. Medicines and drug testing in the workplace. J of Psychoactive Drugs 1990;22:451-9.

20. Jaffe JH. Drug addiction and drug abuse. In: Goodman, L.S. & Gilman, A, eds. The Pharmacological Basis of Therapeutics. New York: Macmillan.

21. A physician's guide to discontinuing benzodiazepine therapy. Western J of Med;152:600-3.

22. Mello NK, Mendelson JH. Operant acquisition of marijuana by women. J of Pham and Exp Therapeutics 1985;235:162-71.

23. Parish DC. Relation of the pre-employment drug testing result to employment status: A one year follow-up. J of Gen Int Med 1988;4:44-7.

24. Members of the Substance-Abuse Testing Committee, Div. of Therapeutic Drug Monitoring and Clin. Toxicology, Am. Assoc. for Clin. Chem: Tai C. Kwong, Ph.D., Chairman, Chamberlain RT, et al. Critical issues in urinalysis of abused substances: Report of the substance-abuse testing committee. Clin Chem 1988;34:605-32.

25. Rothstein MA. Medical Screening and the Employee Health Cost Crisis 1989. Washington, D.C.: Bureau of National Affairs.

26. Laurell H, Tornros J. Hypnotics and traffic safety 1988. In:Lonnerholm G. (Ed.). Treatment of Sleep Disorders. Uppsala, Sweden: National Board of Health and Welfare Drug Information Committee.

27. Sprout WL. Drug screening practices in small businesses: A survey. Occupational Medicine Forum 1988;34:300-2.

28. Honour JW. Testing for drug abuse. The Lancet 1996;348:41-3.

29. Caidin M. Risks of random drug testing. Aviation Safety; June 15, 1993:6-8.

30. McBay AJ. Comparison of urine and hair testing for drugs of abuse. J of Analytical Toxicology 1995;19:201-4.

31. Frye v. United States, 293 F 1013 (DC Cir 1923).

32. California v. Trombetta, 467 US 479, 104 SCt2528, 81 L Ed2d 413, 1984.

33. Silverberg v. Dept. Health and Human Services. U.S. Dist. Ct., DC, civil action, case number 89-2743 (1991).

34. McBay AJ, Mason AP. Forensic science identification of drugs of abuse. J of Forensic Sciences1989;34:1471-6.

35. Hansen HJ, Candill SP, Boone J. Crisis in drug testing: results of CDC blind study. JAMA 1985;253:2382-7.

36. McMillan DE. Urine screening: What does it mean? 1989. In: Harris LS. (ed.) Proc. 51st. Annu. Sci. Meeting 1989. NIDA Res. Monograph 95. Rockville, Md: Natl. Inst. Drug Abuse. 727 pp.

37. Baer DM, Belsey RE, Skeels MR. A survey of state regulation of testing for drugs of abuse outside of licensed (accredited) clinical laboratories. Am J of Public Health 1990;80:713-5.

38. Camara PD, Audette L, Velletri K, et al. False-positive immunoassay results for urine benzodiazepines in patients recieving oxaprozin (Daypro). Clin Chem 1995;41:115-9.

39. Sloop G, Hall M, Simmons GT, Robinson CA. False-positive postmortem EMIT drugs-of-abuse assay due to lactate dehydrogenase and lactate in urine. J of Analytical Toxicology 1995;19:554-6.

40. Trevilla PH, Jimenez EO, Tena T. Prence of Rifampicin in urine causes cross-reactivity with opiates using the KIMS method. J of Analytical Toxicology 1995;19:200.

41. Poklis A, Hall KV, Still J. Ranitidine interference with the monoclonal EMIT d.a.u. amphetamine/methamphetamine immunoassay. J of Analytical Toxicology 1991;15:101-3.

42. Valentine JL, Middleton R, Sparks C. Identification of urinary benzodiazepines and their metabolites: Comparison of automated HPLC and GC-MS after

Immunoassay screening of clinical specimens. J of Analytical Toxicology 1996;20:416-24.

43. Ferrara SD, Tedeschi L, Frison G, et al. Drugs-of-abuse testing in urine: Statistical approach and experimental comparison of immunochemical and chromatographic techniques. J of Analytical Toxicology 1994;18:278-91

44. Huestis MA, Mitchell JM, Cone EJ. Detection times of marijuana metabolites in urine by immunoassay and GC-MS. J of Analytical Toxicology 1995;19:444-9.

45. McNally AJ, Goc-Szkutnicka K, Li Z, et al. An Online immunoassay for LSD: Comparison with GC-MS and the Abuscreen RIA. J of Analytical Toxicology 1996;20:404-8.

46. Kintz P, Machart D, Jamey C, Mangin. Comparison between GC-MS and the EMIT II, Abbott ADx, and Roche Online Immunoassays for the determination of THCCOOH; J of Analytical Toxicology 1995;19:304-6.

47. De la Torre R, Badia R, Gonzalez G, et al. Cross-reactivity of stimulants found in sports drug testing by two fluorescence polarization immunoassays. J of Analytical Toxicology 1996;20:165-170.

48. Matuch-Hite T, Jones Jr. P, Moriarity J. Interference of oxaprozin with benzodiazepines via enzyme immunoassay technique. J Analytical Toxicology 1995;19:130.

49. Joseph R, Dickerson S, Willis R, Frankenfield D, Cone EJ, Smith DR. Interference by nonsteroidal anti-inflammatory drugs in EMIT and TDx assays for drugs of abuse. J of Analytical Toxicology 1995;19:13-7.

50. D'Nicuola J, Jones R, Levine B, Smith ML. Evaluation of six commercial amphetamine and methamphetamine immunoassays for cross-reactivity to phenylopanolamine and ephedrine in urine. J of Analytical Toxicology 1992;16:211-3.

51. Koch TR, Raglin RL, Kirk S, Bruni JF. Improved screening for benzodiazepines metabolites in urine using the TRIAGE panel for drugs of abuse. J of Analytical Toxicology 1994;18:168-72.

52. Hailer M, Glienke Y, Schwab I, Von Meyer L. Modification and evaluation of Abuscreen Online Assays for Drug Metabolites in urine performed on a COBAS FARA II in comparison with EMIT d.a.u. Cannabinoid 20. J of Analytical Toxicology 1995;19:99-103.

53. Poklis A, O'Neal CL. Potential for false-positive results by the TRIAGE panel of drugs-of-abuse immunoassay. J of Analytical Toxicology 1996;20:209-10.

54. Poklis A. Final Critique AACC/CAP Urine Drug Testing (Screening) Survey, UDS-B. College of American Pathologists, Northfield, IL, 1995.

55. McBurney LJ, Bobbie BA, Sepp LA. GC/MS and EMIT analysis for delta-9-tetrahydrocannabinol metabolites in plasma and urine for human subjects. J of Analytical Toxicology. 1986;10:56-64.

56. Kelly P, Jones R. Metabolism of tetrahydrocannabinol in frequent and infrequent marijuana users. J. of Analytical Toxicology 1992;16:228-35.

57. Biochemicals, Organic Compounds for Research and Diagnostic Reagents. Sigma Chemical Co., St. Louis, MO, 1994:485-7.

58. Kemp PM, Abukhalaf IK, Manno JE, et al. Cannaboids in humans. II. The influence of three methods of hydrolysis on the concentration of THC and two metabolites in urine. J of Analytical Toxicology 1995;19:292-7.

59. Sung E, Neeley WE. A cost-effective system for performing therapeutic drug assays. I. Optimisation of the theophylline assay. Clin Chem 1985;31:1210-5.

60. Altunkaya D. Urinary cannabinoid analysis: Comparison of four immunoassays with GC/MS. Forensic Sci International 1991;50:15-22.

61. Chang JY. Drug testing and interpretaton of results. PharmChem Newsletter 1987;16:1-4.

62. Kemp PM, Abukhalaf IK, Manno JE, et al. Cannabinoids in humans. Analysis of delta-9-tetracannabinol and six metabolites in plasma and urine using GC-MS. J of Analytical Toxicology 1995;19:285-91.

63. Foltz RL, McGinnis KM, Chinn DM. Quanitative measurement of delta-9-tetracannabinol and two major metabolites in physiological specimens using capillary column gas chromatography negative chemical ionization mass spectrometry. Biomed Mass Spectrom 1983;10:316-23.

64. Fretthold DW. Drug-testing methods and reliability. J of Psychoactive Drugs 1990;22:419-28.

65. Goldberger BA, Caplan YH, Maguire T, Cone EJ. Testing human hair for drugs of abuse. III. Identification of Heroin and 6-actylmorphine as indicators of heroin use. J of Analytical Toxicology 1991;15:226-31.

66. Sniegoski LT, Welch MJ. Interlaboratory studies on the analysis of hair for drugs of abuse: Results from the fourth exercise. J of Analytical Toxicology 1996;20:242-7.

67. Thurman EM, Pederson MJ, Stout RL, Martin T. Distinguishing sympathomimetic amines from amphetamine and methamphetamine in urine by gas chromatography/mass spectrometry. J of Analytical Toxicology; 1992;16:19-27.

68. ElSohly MA, Stanford DF, Sherman D, et al. A procedure for eliminating interferences from ephedrine and related compounds in the GC/MS analysis of amphetamine and methamphetamine. J of Analytical Toxicology 1992;16:109-11.

69. Hornbeck CL, Carrig JE, Czarny RJ. Detection of a GC/MS artifact peak as methamphetamine. J of Analytical Toxicology 1993;17:257-63.

70. ElSohly MA, Jones AB. Drug testing in the workplace: Could a positive test for one of the mandated drugs be for reasons other than illicit use of the drug. J of Analytical Toxicology 1995;19:450-8.

71. Rollins DE, Jennison TA, Jones G. Investigation of interference by nonsteroidal anti-inflamatory drugs in urine tests for abused drugs. Clin Chem 1990;36:602-6.

72. Allen Jr. LV, Stiles ML. Specificity of the cannabinoid metabolite and phencyclidine EMIT d.a.u. Assays. J of Analytical Toxicology 1988;12:45-7.

73. Fitzgerald RL, Ramos JM, Bogema SC, Poklis A. Resolution of methamphetamine stereoisomers in urine drug testing: Urinary excretion of R(-)-methamphetamine following use of nasal inhalers. J of Analytical Toxicology 1988;12:255-9.

74. Larson J, Forerson R. Nonsteroidal anti-inflamatory drug interferences in TDx assays for abused drugs. Clin Chem 1988;34:987-8.

75. Lorenzen D. Syva letters. Palo Alto, CA: Syva, Feb, March, April, June, July, 1986.

76. Badcock NR, O'Reily. False positive EMIT-st ethanol screen with postmortem infant plasma. Clin Chem 1992;38:438.

77. Thede-Reynolds K, Johnson GF. False positive ethanol results by EMIT. Clin Chem 1993;39:1143.

78. Thompson WC, Malhotra D, Schammel DP, Blackwell W, Ward ME, Dasgupta A. False positive ethanol in clinical and postmortem sera by enzymatic assay: elimination of interference by measuring alcohol in protein free ultrafiltrate. Clin Chem 1994;40:1594-5.

79. Ketchum CH, Stabler TV, Upton KA, Robinson CA. Positivity rate of urine opiate tests following ingestion of poppy seeds. Clin Chem 1990;36:1026.

80. Struempler RE. Excretion of morphine in urine following the ingestion of poppy seeds. Milit Med 1988;153;468-70.

81. Elsohly HN, Stanford DF, Jones AB, ElSohly MA, Snyder H, Pedersen C. Gas chromatographic/mass spectometric analysis of morphine and codeine in human urine of poppy seed eaters. J of Forensic Sci1988;33:347-56.

82. Bjerver K, Jonsson J. Morphine intake from poppy seed food. J of Pharm Pharmacol 1982;34:798-801.

83. Hayes LW, Krasselt WG, Mueggler PA. concentrations of morphine and codeine in serum and urine after ingestion of poppy seeds. Clin Chem 1987;33:806-8.

84. ElSohly MA, Jones AB. Morphine and codeine in biological fluids: approaches to source differentation. Forensic Sci Rev 1989;1:13-22.

85. ElSohly HN, ElSohly MA, Stanford DF. Poppy seed ingestion and opiates urinalysis results: A closer look. J of Analytical Toxicology 1991;36:685-6.

86. Selavka CM. Poppy seed ingestion as a contributing factor to opiate-positive urinalysis results : The pacific perspective. J of Forensic Sci 1991;36:685-6.

87. Fritschi G, Prescott WR. Morphine levels in urine subsequent to poppy seed consumption. Forensic Sci International 1985;27:111-7.

88. Paul BD, Mitchell JM, Mell LD, Irving J. Gas chromatography/electron impact mass fragmentometric determination of urinary 6-acetylmorphine, a metabolite of heroine. J of Analytical Toxicology 1989;13:2-7.

89. Fehn J, Megges G. Detection of O-6-monoacetylmorphine in urine samples by GC/MS as evidence of heroine use. J of Analytical Toxicology 1985;9:134-8.

90. Wick Jr. RL, Brawley WL, Berger BT. A survey of pre-placement urinalisis drug findings. Aviat Space Enviroment Med 1992;63:56-9.

91. Macdonald DI, the medical review officer. J of Psychoactive Drugs 1990;22:429-34.

92. Segura J, de la Torre R, Donike M, Aubets J, Mestres M, Cami J. Value of enzyme immunoassay in the dope control of phenylalkylamines. Proceedings III World conference Clinical Pharmacology. Stockholm, Sweden 1986, p 121.

93. Segura J, de la Torre R. Methodology Evaluation for Urine Drug Testing. Ferrara SD, Sunshine I, eds. Syva Co, Palo Alto, CA, 1987, pp 26-37.

94. Mason AP, Perez-Reyes M, McBay AJ, foltz RL. Cannabinoid concentrations in plasma after passive inhalation of marijuana smoke. J of Analytical Toxicology 1983;7:172-4.

95. Perez-Reyes M, Di Guiseppi S, Davis KH. Passive inhalation of marijuana smoke and urinary excretion of cannabinoids. JAMA 1983;249:475.

96. Perez-Reyes M, Di Guiseppi S, Mason AP, Davis KH. Passive inhalation of marijuana smoke and urinary excretion of cannabinoids. Clin Pharmacol Ther 1983;34:36-41.

97. Ferslew KE, Manno JE, Manno BR. Determination of urinary cannabinoid metabolites following incidental exposure to marijuana smoke. Res commun Substance Abuse 1983;4:289-300.

98. Morland J, Bugge A, Skuterud B, Steen A, Wethe GH, Kjedlsen T. Cannabinoids in blood and urine after passive inhalation of cannabis smoke. J of Forensic Sci 1985;30:997-1002.

99. Cone EJ, Johnson RE, Darwin WD, Yousefnejad D, Mell LD, Paul BD, Mithcell J. Passive inhalation of marijuana smoke: Urinalisis and room levels of delta-9-tetrahydrocannabinol.J of Analytical Toxicology 1987;11:89-95.

100. Cone EJ. Marijuana Effects and Urinalysis After Passive Inhalation and Oral Ingestion: Laboratory of Chemistry and Drug Metabolism, National Institute on Drug Abuse, Baltimore, MD, NIDA Res. Monograph 1990;99:88-96.

101. National Narcotics Intelligence Consumers Committe. Executive Summary: The Supply of Illicit Drugs to the United States. August 1995.

102. Bateman DA, Heagarty MC. Passive freebase cocaine ('crack') inhalation by infants and toddlers. Am J of Disabled Children 1989;143:25-7.

103. Kharasch SJ, Glotzer D, Vinci R, Weitzman M, Sargent J. Unsuspected cocaine exposure in young children. Am J of Disabled Children 1991;145:204-206.

104. Baselt RC, Yoshikawa DM, Chang Jy. Passive inhalation of cocaine. Clin Chem 1991;37:2150-61.

105. Cone EJ, Yousefnejad D, Hillsgrove MJ, Holicky B, Darwin WD. Passive Inhalation of Cocaine. J of Analytical Toxicology 1995;19:399-411.

106. Oyler J, Darwin WD, Cone EJ. Cocaine Contamination of United States Paper Currency. J of Analytical Toxicology 1996;20:213-6.

107. Department of Health and Human Services 1988b. Medical Review Officer Manual-A Guide to Evaluating Urine Drug Analysis. Washington, D.C.:U.S.GPO.

108. Saitoh M, Uzuka M, Sakamoto M. Rate of hair growth. In: Advances in Biology of Skin. Vol IX Hair Growth 1969. Montagna W, Dobson RL, eds. Pergamon, Oxford, pp. 183-201.

109. Henderson GL, Harkey MR, Zhou C. Incorporation of isotopically labeled cocaine and metabolites into human hair: 1. Dose-response relationships. J of Analytical Toxicology 1996;20:1-11.

110. Baumgartner WA, Hill VA, Blahd WH. Hair analysis for drugs of abuse. J of Forensic Sci 1989;34:1433-53.

111. Joseph RE, Su T, Cone EJ. In vitro binding studies of drugs to hair: Influence of melanin and lipids on cocaine binding to causasoid and africoid hair. J of Analytical Toxicology 1996;20:338-44.

112. Green SJ, Wilson JF. The effect of hair color on the incorporation of methadone into hair in the rat. J of Analytical Toxicology 1996;20:121-3.

113. Green SJ, Wilson JF. The effect of hair color on the incorporation of methodone into hair in the rat. J of Analytical Toxicology 1996;20:121-3.

114. Gygi SP, Joseph Jr. RE, Cone EJ, Wilkins DG, Rollins DE. Incorporation of codeine and metabolites into hair: role of pigmentation. Drug Metab Dispos 1996;24:495-501.

115. Slawson MH, Wilkins DG, Foltz RL, Rollins DE. Quantitative determination of phencyclidine in pigmented and nonpigmented hair by ion-trap mass spectrometry. J of Analytical Toxicology 1996;20:350-4.

116. DuPont RL, Baumgartner WA. Drug testing by urine and hair analysis: complementary features and scientific issues. Forensic Sci International 1995;70:63-76.

117. Blanck DL, Kidwell DA. Decontaminaton procedures for drugs of abuse in hair: are they sufficient. Forensic Sci International 1995;70:13-38.

118. Blank DL, Kidwell DA. External contamination of hair by cocaine: an issue in forensic interpretation. Forensic Sci International 1993;63:145-56.

119. Cone EJ, Yousefnejad D, Darwin WD, Maguire T. Testing human hair for drugs of abuse. II. Identification of unique cocaine metabolites in hair of drug abusers and evaluation of decontamination procedures. J of Analytical Toxicology 1991;15:250-5.

120. Baumgartner WA, Hill VA, Blahd WH. Hair analysis for drugs of abuse. J of Forensic Sci 1989;34:1433-53.

121. Potsch L. Stability of opiates in the hair fiber after exposure to cosmetic treatment and UV radiation. Presented at the International Association of Forensic Toxicologists-Society of Forensic Toxicologists Joint Meeting, Tampa, FL, October 31-November 4, 1994.

122. Baiker C, Serrano L, Linder B. Hypochlorite adulteration of urine causing decreased concentraton of delta-9-THC-COOH by GC/MS.J of Analytical Toxicology 1994;18:101-3.

123. Schwarzhoff R, Cody J. The effect of adulterating agents on FPIA analysis of urine for drugs of abuse. J of Analytical Toxicology 1993;17:14-7.

124. Cody JT, Schwarzhoff RH. Impact of adulterants on RIA analysis of urine for drugs of abuse. J of Analytical Toxicology 1989;13:277-84.

125. Mikkelsen SL. Ash KO. Adulterants causing false negatives in illicit drug testing. Clin Chem 1988;34:2333-6.

126. Warner A. Interference of common household chemicals in immunoassay methods for drugs of abuse. Clin Chem 1989;35:648-51.

127. Pearson SD, Ash KO, Urry FM. Mechanism of false-negative urine cannabinoid immunoassay screens by Visine eyedrops. Clin Chem 1989;35:636-8

128. Roth KDW, Siegel NA, Johnson Jr. RW, Litauszki L, Salvati Jr.L, Harrington CA, Wray LK. Investigation of the effects of solution composition and container material type on the loss of 11-nor-delta-9-THC-9-carboxylic acid. J of Analytical Toxicology 1996;20:291-300.

129. Giardino NJ. Stability of 11-nor-delta-9-tetrahydrocannabinol in negative human urine in high density polyethylene (Nalgene). J of Analytical Toxicology 1996;20:275-6.

130. Current Medical Diagnosis and Treatment, eds. Tierney LM, McPhee SJ, Papadakis MA. Lang, Stamford, CT, pp. 1353.

131. Lora-Tamayo C, Tena T, Rodriguez A. High concentration of ciprofloxacin in urine invalidates EMIT results. J of Analytical Toxicology 1996;20:334.

132. Lora-Tamayo C, Tena T. High concentration of metronidazole in urine invalidates EMIT results. J of Analytical Toxicology 1991;15:159.

133. Winek CL, Elzein EO, Wahba WW, Feldman JA. Interference of herbal drinks with urinalysis for drugs of abuse. J of Analytical Toxicology 1993;17:246-7.

134. Turner CE. Marijuana and cannabis research: why the conflict? In: Harvey DJ, ed. Marijuana, 1984. Proc., Oxford symp. on cannibis. Oxford:IRL Press, 1985:31-6.

135. Mechoulam R, Srebnik M, Burstein S. Cannabis chemistry, biochemistry, and therapeutic applications-an overview. In: Harvey DJ, ed. Marijuana, 1984. Proc., Oxford symp on cannabis. Oxford:IRL Press, 1985:1-12.

136. Yesavage JA, Leirer BO, Denari M, Hollister LE. Carry-over effects of marijuana intoxication in aircraft pilot performance: A preliminary report. American J of Psychiatry 1985;142:1325-9.

137. McBay Aj. Interpretation of blood in urine cannabinoid concentrations. J of forensic Sci 1988;33:875-83.

138. Jones RT. Drugs of abuse profile: Cannabis. Clin Chem 1987;33(Supp):72B-81B.

139. Mason AP, McBay AJ. Cannabis: Pharmacology and interpretation of effects. J of Forensic Sci 1985;30:615-31.

140. Wadler GI, Hainline B. drugs and the athlete, F.A. Davis, Philadelphia, 1989.

141. Hunt CA, Jones RT. Tolerance and disposition of tetrahydrocannabinol in man. J Pharmacol Exp ther 1980;215:35-44.

142. Wall ME, Sadler BM, Brine D, Taylor H, Perez-Reyes M. Metabolism, disposition, and kinetics of delta-9-tetrahydocannabinol in men and women. Clin Pharmacol Exp Ther 1983;34:352-63.

143. Dackis CA, Pottash AL, Annitto W, Gold MS. Persistence of urinary marijuana levels after supervised abstinence. Am J Psychiatry 1982;139:1196-8.

144. Ellis GM, Mann MA, Judson BA, Schramm NT, Tashchian A. Excretion patterns of cannabinoid metabolites after last use in a group of chronic users. Clin Pharmacol Ther 1985;38:572-8.

145. Cone EJ. Research findings on smoking of abused substances, 1990. Chiang CN, Hawks RL, eds. U.S. Government Printing Ofice, Washington, DC. Natl. Inst. Drug Abuse Res. Monogr. Ser. 99:88-96.

146. Law B,, Mason PA, Moffat AC, Gleadle RI, King LJ. Forensic aspects of the metabolism and excretion of cannabinoids following ingestion of cannabis resin. J Pharm Pharmacol 1983;36:289-94.

147. Cone EJ, Johnson RE, Paul BD, Mell LD, Mitchell J. Marijuana-laced brownies: behavioral effects, psysiologic effects, and urinalysis in humans following ingestion. J of Analytical Toxicology 1988;12:169-75.

148. Jones RT. The pharmacology of cocaine smoking in humans. Langly Porter Psychiatric Institute, University of California, San Francisco. NIDA Res. Monogr. 1990;99:30-41.

149. Jones RT. The pharmacology of cocaine. In: Grabwski J, ed. Cocaine: pharmacology effects and treatment of abuse. NIDA Res. Monogr. No. 50. DHHS Pub. No. (ADM) 84-1326. Washington, D.C.: Supt. of Documents, U.S., Govt. Printing Office 1982:34-53.

150. Biebuyck JF, Phil D. Pharmacology and therapeutic applications of cocaine. Anesthesiology 1990;73:518-31.

151. Rubin RB, Neugarten J. Medical comlications of cocaine: changes in patterns of use and spectrum of complications. J Toxicology and Clinical Toxicology 1992;30:1-12.

152. Wagner JC. Enhancement of athletic performance with drugs: An overview. Sports Medicine 1991;12:250-65.

153. Leshner A, Head of Nat. Inst. on Drug Abuse at the NIDA Regional Conference. San Francisco, CA. December 2, 1996.

154. Holbrook JM. CNS stimulants. In: Bennett G, Vourakis C, Woolf DS, eds. Substance Abuse: Pharmacology, Development and Clinical Perspective. New York: John Wiley and Sones, 1983.

155. Jacobs MR, Fehr K. Drugs and Drugs of Abuse. A Reference Text, 2nd ed., Toronto: Addiction Res. Found. 1987;1987;183:94.

156. Stewart CH. Barbiturates. In: Gilman AG and Goodman LS, eds. The Pharmacological Basis of Therapeutics, 6th ed., New York: Macmillan Publ. Co. Inc. 1980:349-61.

157. Ravn-Jonsen A, Lunding M, Secher O. Excretion of phenobarbitone in urine after intake of large doses. Acta Pharmacol Toxicol 1969;27:193-201.

158. Kalow W, Tang BK, Kadar D, Inaba T. Distinctive patterns of amobarbitol metabolism. Clin Pharmacol Ther 1987;24:576-82.

159. Budd RD, Walkin E. Mass screening and confirmation of diazepam in urine by EMIT-thin-layer chromatography. Clin Toxicology 1980;16:201-7.

160. Verebely K, Jukofsky D, Mule SJ. Confirmation of EMIT benzodiazepine assay by GLC/NPD. J of Analytical Toxicology 1982;6:305-8.

161. Clouet DH. ed. Phencyclidine: an update. NIDA Res. Monogr. 64. DHHS Pub. No. (ADM) 86-1443. Washington, DC: Supt. of Documents. U.S. Govt. Printing Office, 1986.

162. Cook CE, Brine DR, Jeffcoat AR, et al. PCP disposition after i.v. and oral doses. Clin Toxicology 1982;31:625-34.

163. Chamberlain RT. Legal considerations in drug use testing: Privacy rights, contracts, and wrongful use of test results. J of Forensic Sci 1989;34:1477-81.

164. Griswold v. Connecticut, 381 U.S. 479, 85 S. Ct. 1678 (1965).

165. DeCew JW. Drug testing: Balancing privacy and public safety. Hastings Center Report 1994;24:17-23.

166. U.S. Constitution, 4th Amendment.

167. Jones v. Coughlin, 600 F. Supp 1214 (D. Ct. N.Y. 1985).

168. National Assoc. of Air Traffic Specialists v. The Honorable Elizabeth Dole, No. A87-073 Civil (Dist. AK. 27 March 1987).

169. Requirement that employee or prospective employee take and pass a physical examination as unlawful employment practice violative of Title VII of Civil Rights Act of 1964. 36 ALR Fed 721-33.

170. Offices of Personal Management. Federal employees health and counseling programs: regulatory requirements for alcoholism and drug abuse programs and services for federal civilian employees. Fed Reg 1984;47:27921-2.

171. Witlock v. Donovan, 598 F. Supp. 126 (D.C. 1984) (handicap).

172. Davis v. Buckers, 451 F. Supp. 791 (E. Dist. Pa. 1978) (handicap).

173. Potter BA, Orfali JS. Drug Testing at Work. A Guide for Employers and Employees. Ronin Publishing,1995

174. Peters Tom, Tom Peters on Defense, Drugs, Education, Bay Area Business, pg. 23.

175. Waldholz, Micheal, Drug Testing in the Workplace: Whose Rights Take Precedence?, The Wall Street Journal, November 11, 1986.

176. Miller MA, Neuropsychological assessment of substance abusers: review and recommendations. Journal of Substance Abuse Treatment, 1985;2:5-17.

177. Center for Disease Control, The results of unregulated testing, Journal of the American Medical Association, Apr. 26 1985.

178. Normand J, Lempert RO, O'Brien CP and the Committee on Drug Use in the Workplace:National Research Council,Institute of Medicine.Under the Influence? Drugs and the American Work Force. National Academy of Sciences, 1994.

179. The Associated Press. Survey: Drug Tests No Deterent. The Register-Guard, April 21, 1996.

180. Heyman RB et al and the American Academy of Pediatrics Committe on substance Abuse. Testing for drugs of Abuse in Children and Adolescents. Pediatrics 1996;98(2):305-7

181. Baer DM, Belsey RE, Skeels MR. A Survey of State Regulation of Testing for Drugs of Abuse Outside of Licensed (accredited) clinical Laboratories. American Journal of Public Health 1990;80(6):713-714.

182. Brock DW, Crowley RC. Physician office laboratory follow-up study report: Atlanta: Centers for Disease Control Order #10348, 1985.

183. Crowley R, Belsey R, Brock D, Baer D. Office laboratory regulation: the Idaho experience. Journal of the American Medical Association 1986;255:374-382.

184. Belsey R, Baer DM. Proficiency of office microbiology testing. Clinical Laboratory Medicine 1986;6:345-354.

185. Belsey R, Goitein RK, Baer DM. Evaluation of a laboratory system intended for use in physicians' offices. I. The reliability of results produced by trained laboratory technologists. Journal of the American Medical Association 1987;258:353-356.

186. Belsey R, Vandenmark M, Goltein RK, Baer DM. Evaluation of a laboratory system intended for use in physicians' officies: II. The reliability of results produced by health care workers without formal or professional laboratory training. Journal of the American Medical Association 1987;258:357-361.

187. Robert E. Gladd. Toward Effective and Ethical Drug Abuse Prevention (Thesis work in progress), University of Nevada, Las Vegas Institute for Ethics & Policy. December, 1997.

188. March 1995 Congressional Quartly (Profile of Solomon's reaction to the January 1991 ground offensive against Iraq).

189. Congressional Record, October 6, 1994.

190. Congressional Record, October 7, 1994.

191. Chandler et al v. Miller , Governor of Georgia, et al. United States Court of Appeals for the Eleventh Circuit. April 15, 1997.

192. Del Jones. USA Today, Low jobless rate hinders drug policies. June 20, 1997.

193. Zwerling C, Drug testing. Journal of the American Medical Association, 1994;272(18): 1467-1468.

194. Horgan J. Test Negative--A look at the "evidence" justifying illicit-drug tests. Scientific American, March 1990;262(3):18-22.

195. John Horgan. Your Ananysis is Faulty: How to lie with drug statistics. NORMAL, April 2, 1990.

196. Robbe H, O'Hanlon J, and the National Highway and Traffic Safety Administration. Marijuana and Actual Driving Performance. National Highway safety Adminisratiuon, Nov, 1993.

197. Drug Free Workplace Act (41. USC.701 et seq.) 1988.

198. Simpson D, Braithwaite RA, Jarvie DR, et al. Screening for Drugs of Abuse (II): Cannanbinoids, Lysergic Acid Diethylamide, Buprenorphine, Mehadone, Barbituates, Benzodiazepines and Other Drugs. Annals of Clinical Biochemistry 1997;34:460-510.

199. Moore FML, Jarvie DR, Dimpson D. Urinary amphetamines, benzodiazepines and methadone: cost-effective detection procedures. Medical Laboratory Science 1992;49:27-33.

200. Colbert DL, Gooch JC. An in-house opiate enzymoimmunoassay based ont the Syva EMIT principle. Clinical Chemistry 1992;38:1483-5.

201. Ammann H, Vinet B. Accuracy, percision, and interferences of three modified EMIT procedures for determining serum phenobarbital, urine morphine and urine cocaine metabolite with a Cobas Fara. Clinical Chemistry 1991;37:2139-40.

202. Boeckx RL. User modification of commercial immunoassay kits. Clinical Chemistry 1992;38:1402-3.

203. Stephen Glass. Don't You D.A.R.E. The New Republic, March 3, 1997

204. More Than Just Saying No. Los Angeles Times from Dialog via Individual Inc. August 21, 1997.

205. International Labour Organization, "Working paper on drug and alcohol screening issues in the maritime industry", Interregional Tripartite Meeting of Experts on Drug and Alcohol in the Maritme Industry, Geneva, 29 September-2 October 1992.

206. Morland J. Types of drug testing programs in the workplace. Bulletin on Narcotics. 1993;XLV(2):83-110.

207. Huestis MA. Judicial acceptance of hair tests for substances of abuse in the United States courts: scientifc,

forensic, and ethical aspects. Therapeutic Drug
Monitoring, 1996;18(4):456-459.

208. Gore SM, Bird AG, Ross AJ, Prision rights:
mandatory drug tests and performance indicators for
prisons. British Medical Journal 1996, June
1;312(7043):1411-3.

209. "Sad loser" image of drug users wrong-UK report.
Reuters, London. Nov. 5, 1997.

210. Smith AJ. Editorial:drug warriors claim to be
fighting for america's kids, but are they? Drug Reform
Coordination Network 1997.

211. American Civil Liberties Union. Workplace rights:
workplace drug testing (ACLU Briefer), 1997.

212. Wells VE, Halperin W, Thun M. The estimated
positive predictive value of screening for illicit drugs in
the workplace. Amirican Journal of Public Health.
1988;78:817-819.

213. Spiehler VR, O'Donnell CM, Gokhale DV.
Confirmation and certainty in toxicology screening.
Clinical Chemistry. 1988;34:1535-9.

214. Jussim D. Drug Tests and Polygraphs: Essential
Tools or Violations of Privacy? Julian Messner, New
York 1987.

215. Ligocki KB. Drug Testing: What We All Need to Know.Scarborough Publishing, Bellingham Washington, 1996.

216. McBay AJ. Oversight Hearing on Drug Testing in the Work Force: Hearing Before the Subcommittee on Employment Opportunities of the Committee on Education and Labor. House of Representatives, 100th Congress 2nd session, April 21, 1988 Washinton D.C. No. 100-70.

217. Isikoff M. Federal drug-test method probed for possible flaws. Washington Post, Oct. 25, 1990.

218. O'Hanlon JF. Human factors in Transport Research: "Critical Tracking Test (CTT) Sesititivity to fatigue in Truck Drivers. Academic Press, London 1981.

219. Gitlow S, Barbarians at the Gates. Journal of Addictive Diseases, 1993;12(2):9-21.

220. Shedler J, Block J. Adolescent drug use and psychological health. A longitudinal inquiry. American Psychologist 1990;45(5):612-30.

221. "By the Way." Reason, Aug/Sept 1989:14

222. National Organization for Reform of Marijuana Law. Drug testing for work, 1995.

223. Brookler R. Industrial standards in workplace drug testring. Personnel Journal, April, 1992.

224. Kranzler HR, Stone J, McLaughlin L. Evaluation of a point-of-care testing product for drugs of abuse; testing site is a key variable. Drug and Alcohol Dependence. 1995 Nov;40(1):55-62.

225. Wagener RE, Linder WM, Valdes R. Decreased signal in Emit assays of drugs of abuse in urine after ingestion of aspirin: potential for false-negative results. Clinical Chemistry; 1994;40(4):608-612.

226. Rollins DE, Forensic urine drug testing, 1989;9:9-10.

227. Ed Uthman, M.D. Diplomate, American Board of Pathology, "Drugs of Abuse and Their Detection in Urine," April 1993.

228. Nadelmann, Ethan A. "Commonsense Drug Policy." Foreign Affairs, Vol. 77(1) Jan-Feb 1998.

229. The Associated Press via Individual Inc. "FAA Reduces Alcohol Testing," Washington D.C. January 6, 1998.

230. Lehrer M. Clinics in Laboratory Medicine.1990;10:271-88.

231. Pickworth WB, Rohrer MS, Fant RV. Effects of abused drugs on psychomotor performance. Experimental Clinical Psychopharmacology 1997;5(3):235-41.

232. PRNewswire via Individual Inc. American Bio Medica Expands Scope of the Rapid Drug Screen To Meet Demand from Clinical Markets Detects

Benzodiazepines, Barbituates, and Tricyclic
Antideressants. November 19.1997.

233. Associated Press World News. Mass drug testing of
night-clubbers raises controversy. January 16,1998

234. Sachs SH, schwartz J, Smith G. Maryland Attorney
general Letter, Office of the Attorney General, Oct. 22,
1986:1-30.

235. American Civil Liberties Union, What ACLU Has to
Say About...Drug Testing in the Workplace, American
Civil Liberties Union, New York, 1986.

236. Chen EM, True JM. Recent Developments in
Employee Drug Testing, Civil Rights and Attorneys' Fees
Annual Handbook, 1989, vol. 4.

237. Hoffman, Abbie. Steal This Urine Test. Penguin
USA, 1987.

Glossary

A.C.L.U.: American Civil Liberties Union-The nation's foremost advocate of individual rights--litigating, legislating, and educating the public on a broad array of issues affecting individual freedom in the United States.

Antibody: (immunoglobulins) Proteins produced by B lymphocytes which can combine with antigens such as bacteria to produce immunity.

Barbiturates: A group of sedative drugs derived from barbituric acid.

Benzodiazepines: a group of tranquilizers which have similar pharmacological activities such as reducing anxiety, relaxing muscles, sedating, and having hypnotic effects. Includes Ativan, Librium, Valium, and Xanax

Benzoylecgonine: the principal metabolite of cocaine found in urine and used for detection and evidence of cocaine use.

Blind testing: The practice of submitting urine specimens containing known drugs as if they were routine samples (the testing personnel do not know they are test samples) to determine laboratory accuracy.

Cannabinoids: Refers to a group of more than 60 compounds found in the plant Cannabis Sativa and includes the marijuana metabolites produced in humans. The most extensively studied cannabinoid is delta-9-tetrahydrocannabinol (THC).

Chain of custody: The policies and procedures that govern collection, handling, storage, and transportation of a urine specimen in an attempt to ensure that the results are correctly matched to the person who donated the specimen and that the specimen is not altered or tampered with from the point of collection through the reporting of test results.

Chromatography: A procedure used to identify substances based on differing amounts of migration up a plate after being placed in an organic solvent.

Confirmatory test: a second test which is used to confirm positive results from an initial screening test. The confirmatory test should be, but is not always, done by a method more specific than the screening tests to provide greater certainty that the test is truly positive.

Cutoff level: The concentration of drug in a urine sample used to determine whether a specimen is positive (at or above the cutoff concentration) or negative (below the cutoff concentration). A low cutoff level detects more drug users, but has more false positive results. A high cutoff level will be less sensitive at detecting actual drug use, but less prone to false positive results. Employers and laboratories are generally able to use any cutoff level they wish.

EMIT: Enzyme Multiplied Immunoassay Technology. A brand of enzyme immunoassay by Syva which is the most common drug testing immunoassay.

Enzyme Immunoassay: (EIA) An immunoassay procedure used to identify drugs by attaching an enzyme tag to the drug in question.

False Negative: Report that drug or metabolite has not been detected when drug or metabolite is present in the specimen.

False positive: Report that drug or metabolite has been detected when drug or metabolite is not present in the specimen.

FPIA: Fluorescence Polarization Immunoassay. A type of immunoassay that identifies the presence of a drug by attaching a tag that glows of fluoreces to the drug in question.

Gas chromatograph-mass spectrometry: A method of analysis in which the compounds in a specimen are concentrated to an extract and then heated to a gas. The gaseous compounds are passed through a column and separated based on polarity and weight and then bombarded by high energy electrons which causes the molecules to fragment. The fragmentation pattern (mass spectrum) is used to identify the molecule.

Immunoassay: A procedure used to identify drugs based on the competition between tagged and un-tagged antigen to combine with antibodies. The uncombined, tagged antigen is an indicator that drug is present.

Melanin: Black pigment found in hair, skin, and the choroid of the eye.

Nanogram: (ng) One billionth of a gram.

Negative result: Test results indicating a drug is not detected at or above the threshold of a test.

NIDA: National Institute of Drug Abuse

Opiates: Class of pain killing drugs related to morphine that were originally derived from the opium plant. These include morphine, codeine, and heroin.

Osmolarity: The number of osmotically active particles or ions per unit volume (similar to concentration).

Positive result: Drug detected at or above the threshold level.

Quality assurance: Planned, systematic activities, both operational and organizational, that ensure a testing system routinely produces reliable results.

Reagent: A substance that takes part in a chemical reaction.

RIA (Radioimmunoassay): An immunoassay procedure used to identify drugs by attaching a radioactive tag to the drug in question.

Six-mono-aceteyl-morphine: An unstable metabolite that is unique to the breakdown of heroin. It can sometimes be used to differentiate heroin use from codeine or poppy seed intake.

THC: Delta 9-tetrahydrocannabinol. The major psychoactive cannabinoid in marijuana.

Tolerance: Requiring increasing amounts of drug to produce the same effect.

Index

due process,134-136

E

economics,11,23
educators,34,41
England,15,37
enzyme,72
enzyme immunoasay,75,76
EMIT,75,76
ephedrine,83,100
equal protection under the law,135-136
ethnic,104-108
European,64
experts,19,61,64

F

false negative,60,69,82,112-124
false positive,12,15,16,44,56,84-97
fat,106,115,117,138
Federal Aviation Administration (FAA),26
Federal employee,17,22,43,58,130
Federal government,20,22,32,42-45
female,51
Fen-Phen,86
fine,43
floride,87
fluorescence polarization immunoassay,75
foods,20,61,86,88,134
Fortune 500,15

FPIA,75
fragmentation,81
fraud,4

G

gas chromatograph-mass spectrometer (GC/MS),80-84,87
George Bush, 23,25
golden seal,119
goverment,20,22,24,27,31,32,37,40,44, 47,52,58,59,60,65,90,91,133,136
guidelines,58,59,90

H

Haight Ashbury Free Clinic,61
hair,103-109
harm, 34,37
hash,138
health,14,24,25,27,29,30,31,37,154
health insurance,18,,21,22,31,52,138
heart disease,50,51
hempseed oil,99
herbs,119,120
heroin,15,89,90,107
high blood pressure,,50
high school,32,33
Hispanic,105
Household survey,32
human error,63,84
human nature,37
human psyche,37
hysteria,34,35,40

Ordering Information

To purchase aditional copies of **UR-INE TROUBLE** and protect yourself from being labeled a drug user, send $19.95 per book plus shipping to:

Vandalay Press
P.O. Box 847
Scottsdale, AZ 85252.
Tel: (602) 945-5336

Credit card orders: Call Toll Free (800) 247-6553

Shipping: $3.95 for one book and $1.00 for each additional book.

Sales tax: Please add 5.8% sales tax for books shipped to Arizona addresses.

See Dealer Bulletin for wholesale pricing and terms.